HOW TO WRITE A PARLIAMENTARY SPEECH

PAUL RICHARDS

HOW TO WRITE A PARLIAMENTARY SPEECH

A PRACTICAL GUIDE FOR POLITICIANS AND SPEECHWRITERS

\Bb\
Biteback Publishing

First published in Great Britain in 2024 by
Biteback Publishing Ltd, London

ISBN 978-1-78590-912-2

10 9 8 7 6 5 4 3 2 1

A CIP catalogue record for this book is available from the British Library.

Set in Minion Pro

Printed and bound in Great Britain by
CPI Group (UK) Ltd, Croydon CR0 4YY

FSC
www.fsc.org
MIX
Paper | Supporting responsible forestry
FSC® C171272

This book is dedicated to Sarah, Alex and Ollie.

'Let thy speech be better than silence, or be silent.'

DIONYSIUS OF HALICARNASSUS

'The business of the orator is not to convince, but persuade; not to inform, but to rouse the mind; to build upon the habitual prejudices of mankind (for reason of itself will do nothing) and to add feeling to prejudice, and action to feeling.'

WILLIAM HAZLITT ON WILLIAM PITT THE ELDER

'I dreamt that I was making a speech in the House. I woke up, and by Jove, I was!'

DUKE OF DEVONSHIRE (1833–1908)

ACKNOWLEDGEMENTS

I'd like to thank Olivia Beattie and Ryan Norman at Biteback and Tom Brown at Dods. Good ideas came from Dave Brinson, J. P. Cherrington, Laura Williamson, John Ludlow, Alan Beattie, Bethany Green and Sarah Richards.

I must thank all the current and former Members of Parliament and Members of the House of Lords who have allowed me to help them with their speeches over the years, including half a dozen current members of the British Cabinet.

CONTENTS

FOREWORD BY LORD WATSON OF WYRE FOREST

I've spent more time than is strictly healthy making speeches in Parliament – from the Commons back benches to the lofty heights of a government minister and, rather astonishingly, as deputy leader of the Labour Party. You might assume that after all this, I jump up in the House of Lords with the confidence of a man who's just won gold at the Olympics. Alas, no. The truth is that delivering a parliamentary speech is still as nerve-racking as the prospect of public nudity in the main hall at the Labour Party conference. One slip of the tongue and you find yourself at the mercy of the press, which can be relied upon to pounce on your every gaffe with the zeal of a butcher's dog at a tray of meat.

This is why I was particularly cheered to hear that Paul Richards has put together a guide on how to write a parliamentary speech. The fact that such a manual didn't already exist is as perplexing as discovering the gender-neutral toilets at the offices of GB News. I've known Paul since I could still lace up a pair of ten-hole Dr Martens, and I can assure you he has the rare talent of turning the driest of subjects into something one might enjoy listening to. His book is a lifesaver, a sort of 'How to Avoid Being an Ass in Public' for the political class.

Now, I'm aware that the boffins down in the labs have been tinkering away with something called artificial intelligence, which promises to churn out speeches with the speed and accuracy of a Boris Johnson drinks order in the American Bar at the Savoy. And while the idea of having one's speech generated by a machine is undeniably appealing, particularly when faced with a Friday parliamentary debate, there's something rather soulless about the whole business. A speech written by AI is as palatable as one of those rubber-chicken dinners you have to eat in railway arch restaurants for candidate fundraisers.

The speeches that stick in the mind are those with a bit of human touch, a splash of passion here, a dash of humour there and perhaps the odd mistake that makes one's audience feel that, despite the suit and the title, you're just as fallible as the next guy or gal. AI might be able to assemble the words, but it can't add the sort of sparkle that makes a speech memorable. And believe me, I've heard plenty of speeches that could have used a bit more sparkle – or, failing that, a decent interval for the audience to take a restorative nap.

Paul highlights the peculiar reluctance of the UK's political class to acknowledge the role of speechwriters – a stark contrast to the superstar status they enjoy in the United States. Yet few speeches suffer from the insight of a professional; most are vastly improved by it. There's no shame in seeking such support, especially when speeches should reflect the gravity of our democratic institutions and the people we represent.

So, let us toast Paul Richards, who wisely champions the craft of speechwriting over the sterile allure of AI. Perhaps one day, Westminster will be filled with robots delivering speeches to holograms. But until that day, we'll persist with our human imperfections and occasional oratorical triumphs. Immanuel Kant noted that we must work with 'the crooked timber of humanity', and our speeches should continue to reflect that.

Lord Watson

August 2024

PREFACE

SLIDING DOORS

It was a disaster. It would probably have been better if the speech remained unspoken. If only the Speaker had failed to call the member. How much better that would have been! The problem was the lack of time to rehearse it. The speech-writer had done their best with the time they had, but a few brief, rushed conversations were no match to the task. It started badly, without a clarity of purpose or direction. The joke fell flat, not just because the punchline was mangled, but also because the content was too close to the line. In fact it was so far over the line, the line was barely visible. The numbers came out all wrong, with a 'billion' appearing instead of a 'million'. And who knew it is pronounced 'Beaver' when it is clearly spelled 'Belvoir'?

The anecdote failed to fly because it seemed unrelated to the topic, although it was never terribly clear what the topic was. When the MP turned the page of their tightly typed script, p. 4 became p. 6, with p. 5 lost to history.

Or was it? P. 5 seemed to reappear, decontextualised, distressed and alone, like a child lost in the supermarket. And just as the peroration was revving up, the Speaker called time, cutting the member off mid-sentence. The member sat down to near-silence, wishing the green benches would swallow them up.

It was a triumph. The tea room was abuzz within minutes of the member sitting down. They had spoken with charm and wit, eloquence and humour. The joke about the other side had raised genuine guffaws and already social media was spreading it far and near. At 4 Millbank, the broadcasters were clipping for the evening bulletins.

Time in preparation had paid off. Yes, four or five drafts of a four-minute speech seemed excessive, but the time invested was repaid five-fold. Even the last-minute read-through revealed a couple of places where the text could be tightened. The anecdote chimed perfectly with the main thrust of the speech. The use of signposts guided the member, and the audience, through the three main points of the speech. The clever metaphor shone like a torch in the night. It was timed to perfection, with the final stressed syllable landing as the final second clicked by. The only sound was the *Hear, Hears* reverberating round the chamber, even, begrudgingly, from the other side.

Later, colleagues congratulated the member on their speech (even the ones who had not heard it), but best of all was the constituent in the Co-op that weekend, who repeated back the key line and said how much they enjoyed the speech. 'So nice to hear an MP speaking sense for a change,' they said with a grin.

INTRODUCTION

PARLIAMENT IS THE PROPER PLACE TO PARLER

The Norman Conquest in 1066 brought mixed results. It was bad news for the Anglo-Saxon landowning and ecclesiastical elites who were dispossessed of their land, riches and status, and good news for the Norman French, Bretons and Flemish elites who replaced them.

The Normans, having massacred the last vestiges of English resistance, established a system of government across England and with it the language of the new governors. They brought 'adultery', 'treason' and 'vice', but on the plus side they delivered 'pleasure', 'leisure', 'courtesy' and 'bacon'.

Norman French was this new language of the new political and religious elite, and there are scores of words in English that derive from the business of being in charge: 'bailiff', 'chancellor', 'council', 'minister', 'baron', 'count', 'dame', 'duke', 'marquis', 'prince', 'sir', 'exchequer', 'sovereignty' and even the word 'government' itself. When the British monarch signs a parliamentary bill into law, he or she writes *La Reine le Veult* or *Le Roy le Veult* on the bill itself to show their assent. In and around Parliament, you can see the serjeant-at-arms who runs the place, see the portcullis emblem everywhere and hear about the guillotine in a debate.

However, the most important Norman French word for our purposes is 'parliament', which anyone with a GCSE in French will tell you is derived from the word parler – to speak. This is what Parliament is all about – making speeches. For a thousand years, men, and for a hundred years, women and men, have been taking to their feet to make speeches. It is not for nothing that old-school London cabbies refer to the Houses of Parliament as 'the gasworks'.

The sad truth is that historically most of them have been a bit rubbish. Lacking focus, devoid of interest, overlong, rambling, indistinct, bombastic, insincere, disingenuous and just plain dull. If you watch Parliament for any sustained period, even just for an afternoon on the Parliament Channel, you can witness occasional glimpses of oratorical skill, moments of genius or just fleeting passages of entertainment, elucidation or knowledge. But most of the time, unfortunately, it is pretty dire: the oratorical equivalent of Nytol.

There has never been a golden age of parliamentary oration. Each generation complains about the quality of contemporary speeches and looks backwards fondly to their antecedents. However, the reality is that when we consider some of the truly great parliamentary speeches, from Cromwell to Churchill, what makes them great is usually that they stand out from the crowd. They are great because they capture the national mood, presage a major shift in policy, make or eviscerate a reputation or drip with invective. In short, they are great because they are distinct from the speeches before and after them. Most speeches in Parliament are run-of-the-mill and eminently forgettable, even by the MPs delivering them.

It might be because the MP is unprepared or under-briefed. They may have been told to make a speech by their whips with little notice. They may be arrogant and assume their words will flow like honey. They may have had one or two too many drinks in Strangers' Bar.

This is a crying shame, because it is easy to turn a poor speech into a decent one. There is no magic here, just the application of some simple rules and tricks of the trade. Turning a decent speech into a great one is harder – it may rely on forces beyond the control of speechwriter or parliamentarian. The ancient Greeks, about whom we will be hearing more in the following pages, talked about *kairos*. This might be loosely translated as the moment, the occasion, the right time.

Occasionally, the circumstances transcend the words. Perhaps the most famous parliamentary moment was the Norway debate conducted on 7–9 May 1940, when the war against fascism was going badly. This was an ordinary adjournment debate (a debate at the end of the 'jour', or day) that turned into a no-confidence vote on Neville Chamberlain. The beleaguered Prime Minister won the vote (281 to 200) but lost the argument. The next day he resigned, and Churchill became our wartime leader. Parliamentary speeches shaped the nation's destiny in a very real way.

Most parliamentary debates are not like the Norway debate.

They concern changes to our taxes, by-passes, drains, schools, dentists and the rest of the fabric of the nation. MPs are thrust into the Chamber with scribbled notes and handouts from lobbyists, and their speeches come and go without touching the sides. But to enhance the quality of speeches in Parliament is not hard, it is in all of our interests, and provides the driving mission of this book.

You might ask – does it matter? No one is watching. Few speeches are reported on. The old joke is that the best way to keep a secret is to announce it to the House of Commons. Most speeches are inconsequential, without impact on legislation or the way we are governed. If 600-odd MPs want to gather for a few days a week and make speeches to a couple of dozen colleagues, then should we just leave them to it? We tolerate all manner of eccentric behaviour, from collecting beer mats to trainspotting to nudism, so why not just let them get on with it? They're mostly harmless. Power exists well away from Parliament – in the Cabinet, in the boardrooms of mighty corporations, in the mainstream media, in the nameless denizens of the Establishment – or at least that's how the argument runs.

Not so. The reality is that parliamentary speeches matter because Parliament matters.

There are plenty of good books on how to write and how to deliver a speech. I can recommend Max Atkinson's *Lend Me Your Ears*, or Richard Heller's *High Impact Speeches*. There are great compendiums of speeches: *The Penguin Book of Modern Speeches*, Philip Collins's *When They Go Low, We Go High*, or Yvette Cooper's *She Speaks*. *You Talkin' to Me?* by

Sam Leith explores the enduring power of rhetoric in our modern culture. Yet for MPs new and old, and for their staff, and for the people who write speeches for MPs and peers, there is no official guide and no obvious handbook. Given that the 2024 general election saw a major new intake of MPs, with 335 who have never been an MP before, a new guide is essential.

All effective communication starts with the audience. So, who is this book aimed at? I imagine the person reading this works for an MP. You might be someone charged with writing speeches as a new part of the job or someone new into the job with this as part of your role. You might, in other words, be like me, aged twenty-three, with a new job in Parliament but without much experience other than student unions and NUS conferences. You might be a seasoned old hand looking for some fresh tips. You may be a student of politics, literature, or rhetoric. You may be someone working in another Parliament, looking to compare and contrast your system with ours. You may even be a Member of Parliament seeking out some sound advice (once you've looked to see if you're named in the index).

This book is aimed at those who woke up this morning with 'write speech' on their to-do list. There are plenty of checklists and top tips. Plenty of examples of good speeches. And almost all the examples and case studies are drawn from the Westminster Parliament, rather than the usual fare in other books about speeches: Martin Luther King, John F. Kennedy, Ronald Reagan, Michelle Obama and so on. There's a huge amount to learn from the likes of these, but speeches in Parliament are different from these barnstorming inaugural addresses, platform performances or rallying cries.

Once you get past the parliamentary protocols and arcane language, at their best, parliamentary speeches can stir the soul, raise a laugh or a tear, capture a mood, coin a phrase or lift the nation to greatness.

The quality of our parliamentary speeches should reflect the quality of our politics. Better politics mean better speeches, and conversely, better speeches mean better politics. A parliamentary speech that is artfully crafted, rigorously thought-through, robustly constructed, intelligently argued and delivered with style, wit and technical skill is a sign that all is not lost in our struggling political system. It serves as a bulwark against the rising tide of populist sloganising and the rancid cesspit that is social media.

Parliamentary democracy is the best system, full stop. It is the way we avoid commissars and the gulag, book-burning and the jackboot, rule by anonymous boardrooms and bad people we cannot eject. The system of politics that involves citizens standing for office, getting elected to serve their neighbours and conducting their business through speech and argument not force or violence is the most effective and noble.

As Labour MP Jess Phillips says in her book:

> Politics is the reason that women have the vote, it is the reason that when you break your leg there is a place for you to go and get it fixed … the reason that a man can no longer legitimately rape his wife in marriage. Politics is the

> universal education that exists in the great majority of the world. Politics is the vaccination programmes that rid the world of smallpox, are close to ridding it of polio and are today helping to bring it back from the worst health crisis in many generations.

Politics, in short, is life. Those who say they have 'no interest in politics' may as well say they have no interest in food, air, water, work, play, other people, or themselves.

As Tony Blair told the House in his last speech as Prime Minister in June 2007:

> I have never pretended to be the greatest House of Commons man, but I can pay the House the greatest compliment I can by saying that from the first until the last I have never stopped fearing it. The tingling apprehension I felt at three minutes to twelve today I felt as much ten years ago and every bit as acute. It is in that fear that respect is retained.
>
> Some may belittle politics but we know it is where people stand tall. And although I know it has its many harsh contentions, it is still the arena which sets the heart beating fast. It may sometimes be a place of low skullduggery but it is more often a place for more noble causes. I wish everyone, friend or foe, well and that is that, the end.

For all the hot air and vacuousness, evasion and obfuscation, not to mention half-hearted speeches to a mostly empty Chamber, our Parliament is still the place where the life-changing laws are enacted, where the mighty are brought low, where the lowly can be raised up, and where, on occasion, great oration can make the political weather. This book, alongside the hard yards of drafting, editing, revising and delivering parliamentary speeches, can ensure that your speeches are worth listening to, have some sort of impact and maintain their rightful place in the repertoire of democracy. Better speeches, better politics.

CHAPTER ONE

WHAT ARE THE RULES AND CONVENTIONS?

Parliament, like any debating chamber, has its own rules and conventions, laid down in *Erskine May*. These have evolved over the many centuries that Parliament has sat.

For example, *Erskine May* covers relatively recent developments such as e-petitions, the election of select committee chairs and the idea of 'backbench business'. It also covers ancient conventions of debate and procedure, or what Sir David Natzler, a former clerk of the House of Commons, calls 'the wonderful world of parliamentary procedure at Westminster'.

Erskine May (1815–86) was an actual person who started out as a junior clerk in the House of Commons and published his *Treatise upon the Law, Privileges, Proceedings and Usage of Parliament* in 1844 when Tory Sir Robert Peel was Prime Minister and the Whigs' John Russell was waiting in the wings.

Erskine May is one of those works, like *Das Kapital* or the Bible, from which people quote but few have read cover to cover. It's vast. Sir David Natzler KCB wrote, 'Thomas Erskine May's original work of 1844 was unmistakeably a book, albeit one which would have challenged any reader to peruse from start to finish.' If you're really interested, they recently made *Erskine May* available online, all gazillion words of it.

STANDING ORDERS

Far more useful and manageable are the Standing Orders. Standing Orders are written rules covering the House of Commons and House of Lords. They cover, for example, how the business of the House is organised, how time is allocated in both Chambers and the rules relating to committees. The latest version was published in May 2024 in a handy A5-sized book and formed an invaluable guide to the legions of new MPs after the 4 July election.

As you might imagine, there are lots of Standing Orders, covering how and when to make speeches, how to behave and what happens if you don't. There are now 163 House of Commons Standing Orders for 'public business' and around 250 for 'private business'.

For example, here's a newish Standing Order relating to proxy voting to give you a flavour:

> 39A. Voting by proxy. A member eligible … may arrange for their vote to be cast by one other member acting as a proxy (a proxy vote) under a scheme drawn up by the Speaker in accordance with this order and published by him. A member is eligible for a proxy vote by reason of – 1 (a) childbirth; (b) care of an infant or newly adopted child;

(c) complications relating to childbirth, miscarriage or baby loss; and (d) serious long-term illness or injury subject to the conditions set out in the scheme published under paragraph 1 of this order.

Parliamentarians should know the Standing Orders, and the speechwriter should dip into the sections relating to the conduct of the debates before starting to write.

For example, SO47 covers the time limits on speeches in debates, whereby the Speaker may 'announce that he intends to call members to speak in a debate, for no longer than any period he may specify, and he may at any time make subsequent announcements varying the terms of an announcement under this paragraph'. This means that a carefully time-scripted speech may become truncated with little notice, thus testing the member's ability to think on their feet and self-edit as they speak.

Or SO42, which covers the conduct of a member who 'persists in irrelevance, or tedious repetition, either of his own arguments or of the arguments used by other members in debate'. In such a case of a member droning on with the same points, the Speaker may 'direct him to discontinue his speech', which is a polite way to say the Speaker will tell you to shut up and sit down. This means that the speechwriter must come up with a logical, sequential flow of arguments in a speech, with as much fresh material as possible. This is where local examples from the constituency are most useful, rather than the generic points from the lobbyists' handouts.

CUSTOM AND PRACTICE

A legendary and much-missed former general secretary of the Labour Party is reputed to have said 'it is a rule, but it isn't written down'. What was true of the Labour Party is also true of Parliament. Much of parliamentary procedure has evolved over centuries and is not codified anywhere in the 250 pages of Standing Orders.

This is known as 'custom and practice'. The practice of bills being 'read' three times in both Houses is not in the Standing Orders, for example. Other procedures have developed through precedents such as rulings made by the Speaker and resolutions of the House. There's a seating plan, for example, which is purely convention. Most Parliaments have named seats for members. Ours doesn't even have enough seats for all the MPs. If all 650 turned up at once, some 200 would have to stand or sit on the floor. If an MP wanted to sit next to their friend in the opposition or take a breather on the front bench, even if they are a backbencher, there is no rule that says they cannot.

In June 2022, ahead of a Second Reading debate on levelling up, the Speaker of the House reminded MPs of some of the conventions which they should observe:

> Before I call the minister to move the Second Reading, I wish to remind members of the House's conventions. With a large number of members seeking to participate today, Members will recall that if they participate in the debate they should be present throughout the opening speeches and the

> wind-ups, be present for most of the debate, and, as a minimum, remain in the Chamber for at least two speeches after their own. Also, while we appreciate that interventions are an important part of our debates, if Members intervene repeatedly they are likely to find themselves being called later in the day than might have otherwise been the case. This is so that we all respect others and treat each other fairly and in the best possible way.

So in short, the Speaker is saying observe these guidelines, or your chances of getting called to speak are remote.

For our purposes, here are some of the main rules that you need to obey when speechwriting and speaking.

USING ELECTRONIC DEVICES

You may want to use a script for your speech, to ensure all the points are covered and all the facts are correct. However, the convention is that members cannot read their speeches. Once, if an MP was spotted reading from notes, other MPs would call 'reading, reading' at them to shame them. However, these days, the rule has become somewhat relaxed. *Erskine May* says:

> In principle, a member is not permitted to read a speech, or a supplementary question, but may make reference to notes. Similarly, a member may read extracts from documents but such extracts and quotations should be reasonably short. The purpose of this rule is to maintain the cut and

> thrust of debate, which depends upon successive speakers meeting in their speeches to some extent the arguments of earlier speeches; debate is more than a series of set speeches prepared beforehand without reference to each other.

The new rules even allow for the discreet use of a 'hand-held electronic device' (a tablet or phone, rather than an electric toothbrush or drill, presumably) as an aide-memoire.

So, you might want to use bullet points or cue cards to structure your arguments and key points, but full scripts on A4 sheets of paper are discouraged.

PARLIAMENTARY LANGUAGE

There are various conventions on how to speak in Parliament. There's a certain civil and courteous style that needs to be mastered and written into the drafts of speeches.

For example, the MP should say something complimentary about the previous speaker.

For example, here's Sarah Sackman MP in the King's Speech debate in July 2024: 'Thank you, Madam Deputy Speaker. It is a pleasure to follow the right hon. and learned Member for Fareham and Waterlooville [Suella Braverman].'

Next, the MP must address the Chair, not other Members of Parliament. The debates are conducted 'through the chair', not directly between members. That means that any reference to 'you' only means the person in the Chair – the Speaker or one of their deputies. Everyone else must be addressed in the third person and never, ever by their actual name.

The MP needs to know their constituency and other aspects of their status. The main ways to address a member are as follows:

- If an MP is not of your own party, you address them as the honourable Member for (name of the constituency) or the honourable member opposite
- If an MP is a member of your own party, you address them as my honourable friend
- If an MP is a member of the Privy Council, you address them as either the right honourable Member for (name of the constituency) or my right honourable friend
- There is a pleasing convention whereby lawyers who are King's Counsel (KC) are addressed as the right honourable and learned Member for (name of constituency). As we just saw, this was how Sarah Sackman MP addressed Suella Braverman MP, one lawyer to another
- And those members who have served as commissioned officers in the armed forces are known as the honourable and gallant Member for (name of constituency)

The official rules state that 'learned' and 'gallant' have 'largely fallen out of use', which is a shame. In April 2022, I note that Caroline Lucas, Green MP for Brighton Pavilion, referred to Sir Keir Starmer like this: 'The right hon. and learned member is making a very powerful speech.' So it hasn't entirely fallen out of use.

You can address a government minister as 'the minister' or 'the Secretary of State' if they are one. Or 'the Prime Minister' or 'the Leader of the Opposition'. Also you can use a title such as 'Chair of the Defence Select Committee' if accurate.

Then you must refer to anyone else as 'they', 'he', she' or whatever their preferred pronouns are. The only 'you' is the person sitting in the Speaker's chair. Occasionally, MPs, especially all the new ones, forget the rules and say 'you' to mean another MP, and get told off for it.

To ask a question to the minister during a ministerial statement, the member must 'bob' up and down to catch the Speaker's eye. This means standing up at the end of each member's contribution in the hope of being called by the Speaker. On 19 July 2024, the new member for Milton Keynes Central was called without knowing she was bobbing:

Mr Deputy Speaker:
I call Emily Darlington.

Emily Darlington:
I am sorry, Mr Deputy Speaker, I was not bobbing but I am happy to ask a question. Are you sure it was me you were calling on?

Mr Deputy Speaker:
Please go ahead. The clerks are struggling a bit with new members.

And thus, Emily Darlington got to quiz the minister.

UNPARLIAMENTARY LANGUAGE

Erskine May says that 'good temper and moderation are the characteristics of parliamentary language'.

This advice was overlooked or ignored by Alison Thewliss, the SNP MP for Glasgow Central, in May 2024 when she said to the immigration minister, 'It is hard to know where to start with this complete and utter drivel. The minister comes here today proud of this tawdry, pathetic, self-defeating piece of fascist nonsense [interruption].'

The Speaker did not admonish the member for use of 'fascist', but Thewliss sailed close to the wind.

In July 2010, Tom Watson, the then-MP for West Bromwich East, challenged the Education Secretary, Michael Gove, over cuts to school budgets. This is the exchange between Watson and Mr Speaker:

> *Tom Watson:*
> He can embarrass himself, he can disgrace his party, but what is intolerable is that he has cynically raised the hopes of hundreds and thousands of families. You're a miserable pipsqueak of a man, Gove. You have—
>
> *Mr Speaker:*
> Order. Before we go any further, I must ask the hon. gentleman to withdraw the term that I think he used. I think I heard the term 'pipsqueak'. The hon. gentleman must withdraw that term. It is not appropriate…

Mr Watson:

Out of deference to you, Mr Speaker, I withdraw it.

In previous eras, this moment would have gone largely unnoticed, but in the emergent social media era of 2010, the clip was watched by many millions of people who would never usually follow debates in the House of Commons.

There is a story about Dennis Skinner getting into trouble for saying half the government are crooks, being told to withdraw it by the Speaker and replying that half the government are not crooks. People will swear blind they've seen the clip. It's a good example of the Mandela Effect, whereby people collectively think they've witnessed something they haven't. Alas, the joke is as old as the hills and was not coined by Dennis Skinner.

Refusal to withdraw a comment might lead to an MP being disciplined. For example, the Speaker could 'name' the member. Naming a member means disciplining an MP for breaking the rules. In extreme circumstances, the Speaker can suspend a member who has already been named under Standing Order 44.

There is no definitive list of unparliamentary words. MPs are advised that the question of whether something said is a breach of order depends on the context. As well as the obvious sweary words, the following terms have been discouraged by Speakers down the ages:

- Bastard
- Blackguard

- Coward
- Deceptive
- Dodgy
- Drunk
- Falsehoods
- Git
- Guttersnipe
- Hooligan
- Hypocrite
- Idiot
- Ignoramus
- Liar
- Pipsqueak (which is why Tom Watson got a telling-off)
- Rat
- Slimy
- Sod
- Squirt
- Stoolpigeon
- Swine
- Tart
- Traitor
- Wart

So just to be clear, calling a member a 'warty tart', a 'lying guttersnipe' or a 'drunken ignoramus' is definitely out.

There's a bit of a myth that MPs cannot name 'the House of Lords' out loud, like Voldemort. The convention is that the House of Lords is referred to as 'the Other Place', but the official guidance is that there is no rule banning the phrase 'House of Lords' and no MP has ever been struck by a bolt of lightning for saying it out loud.

If you want to look like you know what you're doing, the MP can refer to the 'Treasury Bench', which means the government front bench in the Chamber.

You're not allowed to sing songs or chant in the Chamber. Occasionally, the strains of 'The Red Flag' have rung out from the Labour benches, notably as MPs voted to nationalise the coal mines in the 1945 parliament and during the no-confidence vote in 1979, when it is said the singing was led by Neil Kinnock. At the high point of drama during the Norway debates in 1940, Labour's Josiah Wedgwood led a verse or two of 'Rule, Britannia', joined by Tory rebels including Harold Macmillan.

Clapping is forbidden too, although MPs are sometimes compelled to applaud when the moment merits it. The Select Committee on Modernisation of the House of Commons stated in 1998 that spontaneous clapping at the end of a speech could lead to the success or failure of a speech being judged not by its argument but by the length of the applause. Craig MacKinlay earned his applause after his appearance in the Chamber after the amputation of his hands and feet after sepsis. As did the Ukrainian ambassador when he appeared in the gallery in 2023. If you want to show approval, you are meant to say 'Hear, hear'. 'Hear, hear' derives from the encouragement by members to 'hear him, hear him' when they agreed with the MP speaking. The shortened version has been in use since the late 1700s, and is still going strong.

SPEAKING ENGLISH

Despite all the Norman French words littering the Palace of Westminster, one important rule is that you must speak English. Many Members of Parliament speak other languages, from Swahili to sign language. But the rules are clear. *Erskine May* says 'speeches in the Chamber and in other proceedings must be made in English'.

That's not to say MPs don't sometimes slip in other languages. Back in 1959, Dingle Foot dropped this into his speech: 'At this late hour of the night, I would commend to ministers who are still on the Treasury Bench, the words of Dr Faustus – *O lente, lente currite noctis equi*.'

Since 1996, the exception is the use of Welsh. This was formalised in a Resolution of the House of 1 March 2017, which states, 'Whilst English is and should remain the language of this House, the use of Welsh be permitted in parliamentary proceedings of Select Committees and of the Welsh Grand Committee held in Wales and at Westminster.' Hansard records both the Welsh language contributions and an English translation, if reasonable notice is given of the proposed use of Welsh.

A rather wonderful breach of the rules happened in March 1993, when Derek Enright MP and Nicholas Fairbairn had the following exchange during a debate on education:

> *Mr Enright:*
>
> What an extraordinary statement. Teachers in any school know best what will fire the imagination and enthusiasm

of their pupils. They use a whole variety of methods to stimulate their pupils – as I did. To help my pupils discover what the optative and subjunctive are all about, I translated Beatles songs into Latin – which would no doubt be to the fury of the hon. gentleman, but it contributed to effective teaching. Many teachers do the same and it is wholly absurd of the hon. gentleman to ridicule teachers who are working effectively at the chalk face, at a job which he could never do.

The Secretary of State talks of giving increased choice, but what increased opportunities for choice do pupils have—

Sir Nicholas Fairbairn:
Will the hon. gentleman give way?

Mr Enright:
I will do so when I have finished making this point, even though the hon. and learned gentleman has only just strolled – I nearly said the wrong word – into the Chamber.

The Secretary of State deliberately refused choice to sixteen-year-olds of the equivalent of the baccalaureate, thereby reducing their choices at eighteen-plus. I give way to the decorously dressed hon. and learned gentleman.

Sir Nicholas Fairbairn:
As a classicist myself with first-class honours, I should be interested to hear a rendition of a Beatles song, with all the words in English translated into Latin by the hon. gentleman.

> *Mr Enright:*
> Certainly.
> '*Habitamus sub vitreo,*
> *Sub vitreo,*
> *Sub vitreo.*'
>
> *Mr Deputy Speaker:*
> Order. The hon. gentleman has been a member of the House long enough to know its rules full well.
>
> *Mr Enright:*
> I apologise unreservedly, Mr Deputy Speaker, but I could not resist the hon. and learned gentleman's challenge.

The rules are there to maintain a high quality of debate, and the Speaker and their deputies are there to see the rules are followed. A member will soon know if they have transgressed the conventions of the House because they will be admonished. Most members soon pick up the language, rhythm, style and pace of the Chamber. For a new member, the best advice is to spend some hours in the Chamber without speaking, just observing and imbibing the conventions and rules.

For the speechwriter, the best advice is to tune into the Parliament Channel frequently and hear how speeches are crafted and delivered, good and bad. You can hear what works and how certain approaches land. As with most things in life, it is about learning by observing what works for others and honing your own craft through practise.

CHAPTER TWO

DRAFTING YOUR SPEECH

When I was a special adviser, churning out ministerial speeches to order, sometimes civil servants would send me something purporting to be the 'draft speech' for the Secretary of State. But usually, it wasn't. It was generally a policy document turned into a series of paragraphs, or even bullet points. The policy would be accurate, up-to-date and resplendent with facts, stats and detail. The civil service is good at that. However, where were the anecdotes, the emotional appeals, the rhetorical questions, the *anaphora*, the tricolons, the alliteration, the metaphors, the *litotes*, the *chiasmus*? Absent was any sense of poetry or persuasion. It was writing for the eye, not the ear. It was not a speech. Policy notes are not speeches.

Incidentally, without getting too pedantic, a speech isn't a piece of paper or a script, and nor is it a video afterwards or the Hansard record. A speech is a speaker speaking to an audience only once. Like a river, which you can't dip your toe in more than once because it has flowed on, a speech is always a one-off. There may be familiar themes or identical sections, but the context is always different because the world has spun on its axis, we are older, even by hours, and things have changed.

What turns a speech into a speech?

SPEECHES ARE LIKE BUILDINGS

My metaphor of choice when it comes to speechwriting is a building. A building has three elements: the raw materials, the architectural structure and the designer's adornments and detailing. A building site with piles of bricks, steel girders and glass is not a building. Nor is a bunch of bullet points of policy a speech.

Even a building with a robust structure – sound foundations, multiple storeys, stairways and a solid roof – may remain merely functional and dull, like those 1960s office blocks that fail to register in your consciousness because they are so boring. When they get demolished, you stare at the empty skyline where once they stood, and you have no memory of them whatsoever. That is most parliamentary speeches: flat, dull, unmemorable. They come and go, and no one remembers what was said.

What creates memorable, compelling speeches? The same as what makes a memorable, compelling building. Impressive, eye-catching design. Attention to detail. Delighting and surprising twists, turns and twiddles.

Consider the design of the Houses of Parliament themselves. Charles Barry and Augustus Pugin designed the new Parliament building after the old one burned down in 1834. It is constructed in the neo-gothic style, mirroring an actual gothic cathedral a few feet away. It is designed to project power and prestige, and it remains a building with the capacity to stir emotions. I first visited the inside of Parliament in the mid-1980s and have been there most weeks ever since. It never fails to have an impact. Once in 1991, Harriet Harman gave me a lift in her car from South London to the House of Commons. As we came over Westminster Bridge, with the morning sun glinting off the tower housing Big Ben, she said, 'It's not bad for the office, is it?'

Yet the impact comes from the attention to detail. Barry and Pugin designed pretty much every detail, inside and out, from the majestic Elizabeth Tower to the skirting boards, chairs, bannisters and CCTV (only joking). It is said that they even put design twirls on the roof that could only be seen from heaven. The fine details are what aggregate the impact of the whole.

A parliamentary speech is no different. The more attention to detail, the better the speech. Yes, you need solid content. You need a strong argument, supported by good evidence. You need a sound architecture. You need to guide your audience around the speech with clear signposts. You need rhetorical devices to stir the soul and lift the spirits.

Most speechwriting books refer to Aristotle's *Rhetoric* as the starting point. This was Aristotle's guide to being persuasive in the Greek *agora*, or public space. If you are fearful of appearing in the *agora*, you are of course *agoraphobic*. The famous trio of modes of persuasion are:

- *Ethos* – the authority or credentials of the speaker
- *Pathos* – the appeals to the emotions of the audience
- *Logos* – the evidence (facts, figures, stats) that support the argument

For a parliamentary speech, you need all three in balance. First, you must establish your credibility, play on the heart-strings and use a few well-chosen and telling facts to support the rational part of your argument.

Here's an example of establishing *ethos*, in an incredibly stark fashion, by Baroness Hayter in a House of Lords committee stage debate in November 2021 on the Police, Crime and Sentencing Bill:

> *Baroness Hayter of Kentish Town:*
> My Lords, I will not repeat what I said earlier about my own mother having been killed because of a drunk driver – though I did not mention at the time that I also lost my brother-in-law in a different accident. The people who did this were not dependent, unregulated drinkers at all; they were perfectly normal people, who got behind the wheel of a car when they had been drinking. As the noble Baroness just said, this is not accidental. It is deliberate: these people have a drink and then get into a car.
>
> But things have altered in those sixty years. I mentioned seatbelts earlier, and there has obviously been the breathalyser. When I first started campaigning on this, the government's

> Christmas campaign that year was 'Stay Low' – it was not even 'Don't Drink'. So we have made enormous progress, and we should not forget that. But it is a journey, and we have not got there yet. We ought to continue on that journey.

This powerful opener gets the attention of their lordships. As well as establishing her authority on the matter, she uses a technique called *paralipsis*, which is where you mention something in passing while denying you are mentioning it. This is how she subtly reiterates the point about her personal experience of the issue at hand.

In the same debate, the crossbencher Baroness Finlay of Llandaff used some *logos*:

> Men are far more likely to have been drinking: 78 per cent of male drivers were involved in drink-drive accidents, against 69 per cent of men in other types of accidents. Where casualties are involved, the numbers are also higher for men – 67 per cent where alcohol was involved, against 60 per cent for all reported accidents.

Harriet Harman used *logos* (as well as rhetorical questions) in this debate on all-women shortlists: 'But how could it have been the result of merit or quality that, when I arrived in 1982, Parliament was 97 per cent men and only 3 per cent women? And this overwhelmingly male parliament was 100 per cent white?'

The raw numbers are so stark and so blatant that they make the argument by themselves.

And here's some *pathos*, from the Green Party's Baroness Jones:

> Many years ago, when I first started getting interested in traffic crime, I went out several times with the traffic police and saw a number of investigations and crashes. At the time, I was told about some incidents that had happened and the sentences that the drivers had got, and these were horrific crashes. A police sergeant working there said to me that if he wanted to kill somebody, he would use his car. He would either get off scot-free or would get a minimal sentence because, finally, you can always claim that it is an accident.

This is an appeal to our emotions; in this case, anger and outrage.

The important thing about *ethos*, *pathos* and *logos* is that you cannot pick and choose between them. Aristotle's point is that you need all three. You can't deliver an effective speech if you have no credibility; you can't rely on sob stories; and you can't just offer the House a blizzard of numbers. You need a skilful blend of reason, emotion and credibility.

The Political Brain by Drew Westen, a US professor, took it one step further and argued that the emotional appeal is stronger than the logical appeal. His studies of the psychological drivers of voting behaviour suggested that people vote with their hearts not their heads. This insight was not lost on those advising the various international populist politicians and movements over the past decade or so, who appeal to fear, hate, distrust and conspiracism over facts, reason, and logic. And those with more noble intentions can use appeals to emotion too.

THE ROLE OF THE SPEECHWRITER

The original professional speechwriters were the *logographers* in ancient Greece. *Logos* means words and *grapho* means write. They wrote legal speeches for the courts. Unlike the USA, there are very few people in British politics with the job title 'speechwriter'. Naturally, however, there are hundreds of people with speechwriting as part of their job description in and around Parliament.

Most parliamentary researchers write speeches for their boss. At least one of the special advisers working for each Cabinet minister writes parliamentary speeches. Civil servants working with ministers provide drafts for their political masters. Many MPs and Lords are writing their own speeches, or at least scribbling some bullet points on the back of an envelope (and sometimes it shows), but many of the words uttered in Parliament are written by someone else.

Yet there is a lingering distaste in the UK for the idea of a speechwriter putting words into the mouths of politicians and a sense that they should be doing it for themselves. I know this from the hundreds of conversations I have had with the best barometer of society's *mores* – London taxi drivers. Usually, on the road from Victoria Station to Portcullis House, Westminster, the conversation goes something like this:

'So, what do you do?'

'I'm a parliamentary speechwriter.'

'Really? Don't they write their own speeches? Lazy sods.'

And from there to roadworks, Nigel Farage, immigration, football or whichever famous politician they once had in the back of the cab.

It is not the same in the USA, where speechwriters have assumed heroic status thanks to their fictional depiction in Aaron Sorkin's *The West Wing* and the real-life personas of US presidential speechwriters such as Pierre Salinger, Peggy Noonan and Jon Favreau. Ted Sorensen ghosted Kennedy's 'Ask Not' speech, the moonshot speech and the bestselling *Profiles in Courage*, which won a Pulitzer Prize (for Kennedy).

They are public figures in their own right. They go on TV and share their wisdom. After their time in the White House, they write books and lecture at universities. They become part of the political firmament without the troublesome business of being elected. It shows the difference in political culture that US speechwriters are famous in political circles (even in the UK), but can you name a single famous British political speechwriter? Who was Boris Johnson's speechwriter? Or David Cameron's? They had them, but they tend to be subterranean, unheralded and anonymous.

One of the few British speechwriters to be known as such is Ronald Millar, who penned some of Margaret Thatcher's most famous words, including 'U-turn if you want to; the lady's not for turning'. This was a pun on the play *The Lady's Not for Burning*, a 1948 drama by Christopher Fry. It is said that the ascetic Mrs Thatcher failed to get the joke.

My first proper job in politics, after being chair of the Labour Party's student organisation NOLS, was for a member of the shadow Cabinet as policy adviser. This was in the lead-up to the 1992 general election. I was working in Parliament surrounded by MPs elected in 1987 or thereafter in by-elections, including the likes of Michael Foot, Tony Benn, Denis Healey, Ian Paisley, John Hume, Edward Heath and Dennis Skinner. I once held the door open for Margaret Thatcher.

Like virtually every parliamentary aide before and since, I was charged with writing speeches for a senior politician infinitely more versed in Parliament, politics and policy than I was. And of course, there was no training programme, mentoring scheme, online resources, or even a handy guide like this one. I don't imagine I was very useful.

Bright young researchers clutching their politics degree certificates are thrown into the deep end without a rubber ring and expected to turn their hand to the skilled job of writing speeches for someone else. They may be experts at writing essays, articles or online content, but few have experience writing a parliamentary speech. It is like asking someone skilled in working with wood to work suddenly with metal. I am sure most would do a half-decent job, adapting existing skills to new tasks, but they would be doing so with neither the right experience nor the correct tools.

So what are these tools? The job of parliamentary speechwriter has many different facets, and it is about more than merely being able to string a sentence together, but that is a good place to start. Oscar Wilde, scrupulous with his writing if not his private life, famously spent the morning deciding to add a comma to one of his poems then spent the afternoon removing it. A successful speechwriter should display a similar degree of attention to detail. We will discuss the techniques used to create a variety of parliamentary speeches throughout this book, but it is worth remembering that this search for the perfect word or phrase, considering not only how they look on the page but how they arrive in the ear, is much of the job. Like any decent writer, the speechwriter must be in love with language, have a passion for poetry and prose and be a perfectionist to the point of obsession.

GHOSTWRITER

You may be a good or even a great writer, but are you a ghostwriter? Up to this point, you may have written prize-winning essays and clever, insightful articles for political magazines, newspapers or websites, or even speeches for yourself to deliver. You can deploy imagery and metaphor, anecdote and allusion, *anaphora* and *anadiplosis*. You can spot a *chiasmus* from 500 paces and know your alliteration from your *zeugma*.

Now, you must develop a different skill – to write in another's voice, capturing their tone, their lexicon, their accent, their experiences, their stories and their jokes. You are like a medium, channelling the voice of another.

The art of writing a speech for someone else is that it must sound authentically like them, not you. When MPs are reading out the scripts prepared by external organisations or their researcher, or when ministers are reading out their civil service briefing, we can spot it a mile off.

Robert Harris's *The Ghost* is the tale of a ghostwriter for a thinly veiled Blair-esque character. Each chapter is headed with a quote from Andrew Crofts's book *Ghostwriting*, which is the definitive guide to writing for other people. Crofts's prodigious career, like Harris's ghost, rests on writing books for people with the desire to tell their stories but without the talent, time or inclination to do it themselves. A passage in *Ghostwriting* has always struck me as containing an interesting psychological insight:

> Many people take up writing because they have powerful opinions that they wish to convey to the world. Such people will find ghosting hard, since it is largely about conveying other people's views – whether you agree with them or not. If you prefer voicing your own opinions to listening to other people's, you might find the ghosting process uncomfortable since you will constantly be wanting to interrupt them and take the floor for yourself…

Andrew Crofts makes the point about conveying views with which you personally disagree. I am often asked if I would write a speech for a politician in a different party to my own, and I would not. But I have often had to make an argument in a speech with which I personally disagree. Like all the ghosts in politics – those writing op-eds, manifestos, policy briefs or speeches for others – the personal is sublimated to the greater task at hand. It is a good mental discipline to be able to articulate an argument with which you might not personally agree and certainly a good way to make sure the argument stacks up.

If you feel compelled to put yourself into the speech – your ideas, passions and voice – you are not going to write a decent speech. Of course, part of the role of speechwriter is to bring ideas, content and even policy to a speech. There is a place for creativity, especially if the politician is a little unclear on what they want to say in the speech. Indeed, part of the fun of being a speechwriter is shaping the edges of policy or highlighting certain areas that might otherwise go unsaid.

But the end result – the speech itself – must sound like them, not you.

Famously, Gordon Brown was lambasted by Michael Heseltine for his use of the phrase 'post-neoclassical endogenous growth theory' in a 1994 speech. Ed Balls got the blame (It's not Brown's, it's Balls'). The idea was that Balls, the economist, had shoehorned a phrase into the mouth of Brown, the politician, that rang untrue. Like most political folklore, that's not quite what happened. Balls and Ed Miliband removed the phrase from the draft speech, but Brown put it back and then said it out loud. Even then, the exact line was 'you wouldn't expect me to talk about post-neoclassical endogenous growth theory', which is, as any speechwriter can tell you, an example of *paralipsis*. No matter; the damage was done.

The only sure route to achieving this is to listen to the parliamentarian speaking. This happens in two ways: in the face-to-face discussion about the speech beforehand, where you may hear good ideas, thoughts or even just a key word or phrase; and when they are giving speeches in a variety of settings. That means you must insist on 'face time' (in the original, not digital, sense) with the MP if you are the writer, and if you are the parliamentarian, you must make time in your diary for your speechwriter.

By tuning into their voice, internalising it and developing the ability to hear it in your head, you can successfully ghostwrite for them. Hearing your MP's voice in your head is definitely a non-transferable skill, but it is essential to the task of speechwriting. You can't write a speech for a stranger.

THE THREE FACES OF THE SPEECHWRITER

Face one – researcher

I seem to recall that every fact or figure that ever appeared on the lips of the fictional President Bartlet in *The West Wing* had been checked against three separate and independent sources. I'm not sure the same was true of real President Trump. In real life, it is a good idea to ensure every fact and figure in your speeches has at least some modicum of veracity. This means that it should be up to date and drawn from a source more reliable than some website you discovered while googling.

The best source of information available to you is the House of Commons Library and the talented researchers they make available to MPs, delivering both bespoke briefings and their off-the-shelf briefing notes. Next, your political party will supply briefings for debates, but beware, these will be the same for everyone, so you might end up making points that sound similar to your colleagues'.

There are dozens of reputable think tanks occupying every inch of the policy and ideological field. Each of these is keen to be mentioned in parliament and may be able to help with bespoke briefing. This is also true of the public affairs people – either in-house or agency – working for NGOs, charities, business trade bodies, trade unions, universities and big companies. If the debate is about an international issue, there may be campaigning organisations and embassies keen to engage with you. There is no shortage of material – the skill is in shifting and sorting what you want to use, what will stand up to scrutiny, what advances your argument, and what is different and distinct.

Face two – clairvoyant

Obviously, there is no such thing as clairvoyance, but the parliamentary speechwriter should always attempt to gaze into the crystal ball and predict the circumstances of the speech. If you can capture something of the time and place in a speech, it will add to its freshness and immediacy.

For example, take a look at the diary and see on which date the speech is down to be delivered. Is there some significance to the date? Is it St Valentine's Day? St David's Day? Chinese New Year? Rosh Hashanah? Stephen Lawrence Day? The eve of England playing in the World Cup final? If the audience are aware of the significance of the day, but the MP fails to mention it, it may look a little remiss.

Is the date the anniversary of some event? Is it ten years or one hundred days since something significant happened? Is it the six-month anniversary of the minister promising to do something they haven't done? Is it a notable person's birthday? Will it be the day after a by-election or the morning of the unemployment figures? Any of these may form the peg for the speech, or least be worth a mention. Then there are the multitude of awareness days, weeks and months, each one important to someone, somewhere. There are various websites which list these.

As well as time, you can consider place. Obviously, a parliamentary speech will only be delivered in the House of Commons or Lords, but who is in the gallery? Have some significant figures been invited to hear the speeches? The speech should mention them. For example, the victims of the Horizon scandal and the contaminated blood scandal were invited to hear MPs from the gallery.

The speechwriter must place themselves into the future time and place that the speech will be delivered in order to best consider the context in which it will be received.

Face three: mind-reader

You need to know the mind of the person you're writing for (or yourself, if you're the parliamentarian). This requires you to make time to discuss the speech in advance and think about the theme, key ideas, stories, jokes and the rest of the content. The writer needs to hear the thoughts of the speaker. I know that in the reality of Parliament, this is sometimes a luxury. The speechwriter needs to work with the diary manager to make time, well in advance, even if it's in the back of a car or on a train.

It might just be a word or phrase that triggers a great passage.

Knowing the mind of the parliamentarian comes with time spent with them. A successful speechwriter will volunteer to spend time with their boss whenever and wherever possible, to tune into their voice, phraseology, the rhythms of their speech and the words or phrases they struggle with. If there's a phrase or word that causes grief, the writer can avoid it next time.

THE RELATIONSHIP BETWEEN SPEECHWRITER AND SPEECHMAKER

There should be a symbiotic relationship between the person writing the speech and the person giving it. The parliamentary researcher should have a close and productive relationship with their boss. The MP should have trust in the quality and accuracy of what they're presented.

A great parliamentary speech is a collaborative effort, with each party bringing something different to the table. The writer brings their writing and editing skills, a fresh take on issues, the latest research and their political nous, and the MP brings their experience, their passion, their authentic voice and their oratorical skill. The writer could not give the speech, and probably the speaker could not write it (although some MPs are great speechwriters too).

THE WRITING PROCESS

Writers need a process. As a special adviser, I used to joke (not really a joke) that I seldom started to write a sentence without being interrupted before finishing it. As an MP's researcher, I recall the same. Life in politics is a constant battle with people who want your attention.

To write a speech, you need to find some time and space to focus. You see people trying to write sitting on the tables by the despatch cafe in Portcullis House. This is a disaster, because you will see people you know, or want to know, every few minutes. You need, like Virginia Woolf, a room of one's own. Some writers like to write to music, with Mozart stimulating and stirring the little grey cells. Others imbibe a dose of great writing before picking up the pen to give them a sense of rhythm and grandeur. Try Milton, Shelley or a contemporary great like Christopher Hitchens or Joan Didion. Your Second Reading debate speech on public lavatories may not require the grandeur of a Shakespeare soliloquy or a Miltonic sonnet, but a little inspiration can go a long way. Certainly, you should never write cold, or else your writing will be bloodless and flat. Uninspired speechwriters write uninspiring speeches.

There's a useful staged writing process called the POWER method. This mnemonic is especially helpful for speechwriters.

P – planning
O – organising

W – writing
E – editing
R – reviewing

The planning stage is a creative, open phase, with the parliamentarian and speechwriter discussing themes, ideas and things to include. The writer can use desk research (especially previous speeches in Hansard and the party briefs), as well as broader research into what relevant people are saying.

As a sidebar, if you are a campaigner or lobbyist, this is a great way to influence the public discourse. Ahead of a Second Reading debate or a Westminster Hall debate, the speechwriter is looking for ideas, new information and case studies, and if you can supply useful information, you may well find yourself quoted in Hansard.

Then comes the organising. This is about taking a scalpel to your material and chopping stuff out. Populate a clear structure with data, anecdotes, a telling metaphor, rhetorical questions and the rest of the tools in the kit. Use clear headings and signposts. Build in the elasticity so that the MP can adapt to the Speaker limiting the time allowed for the speech. Some people do it on screen, some people use Post-its or just paragraph headings jotted in their Moleskine notebook.

Then the writing. The advice here is to just splurge it onto the screen or page. Don't worry too much about accuracy or getting every word right. Just get it from your head and onto the page. The crucial point here is that you can't plan, organise and write at the same time. That only leads to overly long sentences, confused arguments and a rambling speech.

The reason for splurging is that you come next to the editing. Here, you hone the phrases, stress-test them out loud, double- and treble-check the facts, build in signposts and ensure the theme sings out. The good news is that you don't need to worry too much about spelling, punctuation or the rules of grammar, because a speech is about sound, not whether the apostrophe is in the right place.

Reviewing is not about that final review before delivery. Reviewing is reviewing after the speech has been delivered. Did it work? What didn't work? What can be improved next time? Part of the speechwriter's role is giving helpful feedback as well as supportive post-match commentary. The researcher or speechwriter must tread a difficult line here between offering constructive comments and being disrespectful. You could use the famous shit-sandwich formula whereby the first thing is positive, the second critical, and the third is positive again.

THE SIGN-OFF PROCESS

There is a moment when the drafting is over and the speech needs to be locked down. Of course, a speech isn't a speech until it's being delivered in the Chamber, but the substantive arguments and policies are not a matter for ad-libs. A speech is like a series of musical notes that can never be played again, but the melody can be established in advance.

You need a sign-off process. This passes responsibility for the content of the speech to the MP, with whom the buck stops.

The process, in an absolutely perfect world, should work something like this:

1. Broad discussion of the key themes, ideas, arguments and content
2. Writer produces first draft
3. MP reads first draft and offers feedback
4. Writer redrafts second draft
5. Read-through with MP, a 'table read' out loud
6. Writer redrafts third draft
7. MP rehearses third draft out loud
8. Final edits based on rehearsal
9. Final rehearsal and speech lock-down
10. Speech delivered
11. Great reception, plaudits from colleagues, positive write-up in the papers

In reality, it often goes something like this:

1. Vague idea to make a speech
2. Rushed conversation on the way to a parliamentary reception
3. Some bullet points on a couple of pages
4. Crazed scribbling in the Chamber
5. Speech delivered
6. Tumbleweed

The fact is that the more time spent in rehearsal and editing, the more effective the speech will be. An effective parliamentary assistant should insist on time in the diary, well in advance, to go through the speech. This may seem like a luxury in the busy day of an MP, but it pays off in spades.

MAKING AN ARGUMENT

When it comes to the content of a parliamentary speech, it is predominately a matter for the MP. No '*How to...*' guide can help you here. The MP should have plenty of things they are passionate about, things they want to change, constituents they want to champion and wrongs they want to right. If not, why are they there? The Liberal MP, then Labour MP (and also founder of the Commonwealth Party) Richard Acland wrote a neat little book called *Public Speaking* in the 1940s. In it, he says, 'You must know what you are talking about before you can talk about it. A burning resentment against current injustices and a woolly aspiration towards the brotherhood of man will not serve as the basis for a public speech on anything.'

In other words, you need an argument.

When I wrote speeches for the Secretary of State for Health Patricia Hewitt, she would usually ask, 'What's the argument?'

- What are you trying to say?
- What is the main thing you want to get across in the speech? Seek to answer the question 'what is this speech going to be about?'
- What is the main dividing line with the other side?
- What examples, illustrations or constituency perspectives will add to your argument?

Given how short parliamentary speeches are becoming, there is an obvious need for clarity and concision in speechwriting. This means making fewer points and being prepared to chop bits out. A successful parliamentary speech is written with a chisel, not a pen.

You need a clear message, one which is compelling, powerful, supported by evidence and can be recalled afterwards by the listeners. You should be able to fit it on a Post-it note. One of the key roles of the speechwriter is stopping a speech from being overloaded. In the drafting and editing, very few people want to remove material and most people want to add stuff in. This is especially true in a ministerial office where there is always a good reason to add more and more material. I compare it to a Christmas tree onto which everyone wants to add baubles. Eventually, the tree is overloaded and topples over. The same is true of an overloaded speech draft. Speechwriting is definitely a method of communication whereby less is more. In his *On Writing*, published in 2000, Stephen King argues that the second draft is the first draft minus ten per cent. This is surely right? An editing process that adds rather than subtracts from the speech has failed.

Erskine May says:

> If any member strays from the question under discussion, the Speaker will intervene to remind that member to speak to the question. If a member persists in irrelevance or tedious repetition either of their own arguments, or of the arguments used by other members in debate, Standing Order

> No. 42 empowers the Speaker, after calling the attention of the House to the member's conduct, to direct them to discontinue their speech.

So, the least we should expect is the avoidance of 'irrelevance or tedious repetition'.

The Speaker or Deputy Speaker will soon step in if the MP is wandering off topic. Here's Rosie Winterton telling off David Linden for straying away from the subject under discussion: 'Order. I assume the hon. gentleman will be coming back to the motion before us.'

Churchill is said to have dismissed soups and puddings if he felt they 'had no theme'. The same is true of speeches. They need a theme. This is the argument that runs through the speech like the word BLACKPOOL through a stick of rock. You can achieve this through repetition of key phrases, through apposite anecdotes, through rhetorical questions, and through supporting evidence.

Context matters too. Consider what is in the news, what is happening in the policy world, what recent announcements have been made, and what's happening in broader society. What's happening in popular culture? Liaise with the casework team and see what the big inbox issues are. You may be surprised when you discover more people are concerned with pylons than the Middle East. Use your powers of clairvoyance to predict what will be in the minds of the audience on the allotted time and day. You need to link your argument to what's going on in the world and what people are thinking about.

The following speech delivered by Lord (Tom) Watson in the House of Lords has a clear theme. If you asked a listener what the speech is about, they would doubtless say it is about the need for the UK to have an industrial strategy and that it questions why we do not have one. It uses quotations, appeals to experts, specific topical examples, rhetorical questions and repetition, and these all add up to a clear theme. Note how Tom Watson links his theme to the events of the week, which were the threats to steel jobs in South Wales.

> This motion would not be debated in the legislative assemblies of the major economies: not in Germany or the USA, nor France, Japan, China, South Korea, nor any other developed nation on earth. Why? Because as the manufacturing trade group Make UK says, the United Kingdom is unique among advanced economies in not having an overarching, comprehensive industrial strategy.
>
> I know that the minister will point to the government's plan for growth, introduced under the previous-but-one Prime Minister in March 2021. I suspect he will want to advance the argument that the plan for growth, with its specific focus on five areas of economic activity, constitutes a strategy. I am sure he will be keen to mention the £500 million per year that the government have earmarked for 20,000 R&D businesses, along with £650 million for life sciences. Let me say at the start that these are all commendable initiatives, and worthwhile in their own right, but they do not yet form part of an overarching strategy. I know that

because, in June 2023, the then minister in the Lords said, 'I think noble Lords will agree that this is a time for specialisation rather than a single, overarching, broad strategy.'

I disagree with that assertion.

I do not think we are doing enough to make a decisive difference to the UK's economic prospects, given our sluggish growth, flatlining wages, regional disparities and chronic underinvestment. I invite the minister to cogitate on why it is that the UK is unique in not having an industrial strategy, while reminding colleagues that a plan is definitely not a strategy. We have had a plethora of announcements, initiatives and institutions since 2010 and a constantly changing cast list: those thirteen years have seen eleven growth strategies, nine Business Secretaries and seven Chancellors. This is partly, I am sure, why Make UK has said that 'a lack of a proper, planned, industrial strategy is the UK's Achilles heel'.

Meanwhile, the Centre for Economic Policy Research reports on the renewed interest within our competitor nations in 'effective tools and strategies to promote economic development and address new challenges, from supply chain risks to national security and climate change'.

It further says that industrial policy has featured significantly in the world's largest economies. Again, I ask the minister: why is the UK the odd one out?

What then is the case for an industrial strategy? An industrial strategy would 'help young people develop the skills they need to do the high-paid, high-skilled jobs of the future. It backs our country for the long term: creating the conditions where successful businesses can emerge and grow and helping them to invest in the future … it identifies the industries that are of strategic value to our economy and works to create a partnership between government and industry to nurture them … it will … propel Britain to global leadership of the industries of the future – from artificial intelligence and big data to clean energy and self-driving vehicles.'

Those are not my words; they are the words of the then Prime Minister, the right honourable Member for Maidenhead, in her foreword to her government's *Industrial Strategy* document in 2017. It is hard to disagree with that, and even harder to understand why the government cancelled it so soon afterwards. It is quite a head-scratcher.

Ministers also abolished the Industrial Strategy Council in 2021. It included Andy Haldane from the Bank of England, the Community union's Roy Rickhuss and ceramicist Emma Bridgewater – all of them were given their marching orders. If you do not have an industrial strategy, you do not need an Industrial Strategy Council to guide it. The respected Institute for Government states, 'Weak productivity performance and regional imbalances have worried politicians for a long time, as has a sense that the UK does not make enough of its abundant strengths in science. These alone are important justifications for an industrial strategy.'

The case is overwhelming. It is why the cry has gone up from trade union leaders, former Conservative and Labour

Cabinet ministers, civic leaders, entrepreneurs and investors. It is no wonder that 99 per cent of British manufacturers back the need for an industrial strategy, and yet we do not have one.

Thankfully, we have a lot to build on. On manufacturing, *The Economist* recently reported a survey of the public that asked respondents to state where they thought the country ranked in global manufacturing league tables. The median answer was forty-third, which was wrong. The latest comparable data makes Britain the world's eighth-biggest manufacturer. *The Economist* said, 'Many manufacturers believe that the successes of recent years have come about despite rather than because of government policy.'

What would a new industrial strategy look like? My starting point is that an effective industrial strategy is not about picking winners or propping up losers, or meddling in markets when they work, and it is not about ministers interfering in the business of business. It is about working in partnership with firms to identify problems and fix them; to see opportunities and seize them; to ask not why but why not.

The moon landing in 1969 needed a strategy that included not only aeronautics but electronics, nutrition, product design, computer software and engineering. The UK right now needs to define its moonshot equivalent. It could be fixing the climate crisis, although we know that is a global challenge. It could be that we are the first country in the world to have a sovereign quantum computing facility. It may be that we choose to build homes for everyone before they are thirty and orient things around that. My point is that there should be a small number of clearly understood and defined national goals where there is currently a vacuum. I am greatly influenced by the work of the economist Mariana Mazzucato, who said, 'Industrial strategy thus holds a dual promise: helping to address climate change and revitalising industry so that it can compete in the twenty-first century. We need not accept … a trade-off … The two can go hand in hand if green policies are deployed to fuel growth and innovation, and if sustainable practices are woven into the fabric of how we consume, move, invest, and build.'

A new industrial strategy would take full cognisance of the UK's context. We have a growing and ageing population, and a huge wealth of talent and expertise in science, technology and manufacturing. We have world-class universities and fantastic entrepreneurs and inventors. We are a global leader in creative industries – gaming, film and music – and native speakers of the English language. We are a great nation, straining at the leash to be allowed to get ahead. It would view climate change as both an existential threat as well as an opportunity for economic growth and technological advance, leading the way in carbon capture, renewable energy and post-carbon manufacturing of everything from hydrogen to nuclear, and from electric vehicles to the next generation of batteries for our phones. It would negate the need for a Department for Levelling Up because it would promote economic activity and growth in every nation and region, not just the south-east and London.

It would provide a stable platform for long-term investment and sustained growth instead of political chopping and changing, which business always tells us is the drag anchor on its success. It would represent a true partnership with small and medium enterprises, growing companies, unicorns, long-established British businesses and government at every level of our devolved constitution. It would allow businesses to thrive, turn profits and create decent, well-paid jobs, and it would allow the state to invest these products of growth into our public realm and shared services. Without economic growth, we do not grow as a society. It would allow the next generation to grow tall.

In my peroration, I will highlight one area where the absurd absence of an industrial strategy is most keenly felt and where the price is most heavily paid: the steel industry. Unless we act soon, the UK will lose its ability to make primary, or virgin, steel for ever.

We will be the only advanced nation unable to make steel, in a time of global turmoil and uncertainty. This would represent criminal negligence. I note the announcement that Tata will close the two blast furnaces at Port Talbot in a few months and install an electric arc furnace, which would cut productive capacity. This is mindless vandalism to our manufacturing base. The salt in the wounds is that the government are throwing £500 million at Tata, to lose 3,000 jobs in steel manufacturing. British Steel in Scunthorpe is looking to close its blast furnaces. These twin actions will mean that we have to import primary steels, with huge costs to the environment.

The trade unions have a plan to transition to cleaner, greener steel production and safeguard local jobs. Community union and the GMB have a workable, serious plan. Is the minister aware that Tata indicated that this plan is credible and viable but was rejected by the government on the grounds of cost? Can he comment on the exact nature of the £500 million offered to Tata, and whether this is in any way related to Tata's battery plant in Somerset? Does the minister know that electric arc furnaces cannot produce the base steel that is needed for tin manufacture – yet 30 per cent of Port Talbot's output is for tin cans? It has the orders, but the means to fulfil them are being removed. Has he read the rescue plan?

I do not want to make the case just for saving jobs in this part of Wales, nor focus on the bitter human cost that will be paid by working people and their families in these proud communities. I do not want to point out just that 20,000 jobs in the supply chain rely on this plant. I am sure others will want to point out the similarities with the destruction of our manufacturing base in the 1980s, with the price paid by miners, steel-workers and skilled engineers and their families in that dark decade of deindustrialisation and demoralisation of whole towns and cities. I want to link what is going on with steel today with my central argument for the need for an industrial strategy.

> An industrial strategy must seek answers to the central questions of our age: our negotiation with rapid technological change, our need to decarbonise, our desperate need for growth and the big shifts in our society. An industrial strategy can mitigate the risks, manage the transition and soften the hammer-blows that rapid change can bring. This is not top-down statism, but it is not free-market fundamentalism either; it is a true partnership with communities, companies, industries and government.
>
> An industrial strategy must view the steel industry as part of a bigger landscape of manufacturing, and manufacturing as part of a bigger landscape of economic activity. It must view economic activity as the basis of our society, culture, well-being and national character. All the moving parts interact and interrelate, just as all humans do. What happens in Port Talbot, in Scunthorpe, in the long-ignored corners of our country and in the left-behind towns and estates happens to us all. This is an essential truth that the government seem to have missed. I beg to move.

If you can't answer the question, 'What is this speech about?', then it is about nothing. A good speech is like a good pencil. It must have a point.

FACTS AND FIGURES

One thing you will not be short of is facts and figures. Every lobbying group, academic study, think tank, trade union, trade body, NGO and government department will be vying for the attention of the MP with their facts and figures. The trick is the curation and selection of facts and figures to make the speech stronger, not more confusing. Choose facts, stats, and numbers that stand out, cause a sharp intake of breath, are surprising or shocking and that we may not have heard before.

Here's an example of two ways to use figures in the Chamber. It's Treasury questions, with Bim Afolami MP being quizzed on the value of co-operatives by Jim McMahon MP:

> *Bim Afolami:*
> The government acknowledge the vital contribution that co-operatives make to the economy. The 'Co-operative and Mutual Economy 2023' report found that co-operatives generated a combined annual turnover of £41 billion, a 3.7 per cent increase from 2022 levels.

> *Jim McMahon:*
> As the minister outlines, co-operatives are worth £41 billion to the UK economy; moreover, they are, on average, 10 per cent more productive than other businesses, twice as likely to survive the first five years of trading and have higher rates of investment than other private businesses. What more can the government do to encourage more co-operatives to thrive? Does he believe, as I do, that the creation of co-operative development agencies in every region has to be part of that?

McMahon echoes the '£41 billion' figure because that's the

figure, but he then adds to his argument with '10 per cent more productive', 'twice as likely to survive' and 'higher rates of investment'. These are easy to understand figures that make the point.

The problem with some debates on specific topics is that the same lobbying groups send the same briefings to friendly MPs, who then read out the same numbers, so try to use evidence that no one else has got or has said. Or at least try to get it in at the start of the debate before everyone else piles in.

SOUNDING AUTHENTIC

There is a real premium in authenticity. We crave 'real' politicians with real-life experiences, backgrounds and stories to tell. We want our political leaders to be sincere. As long ago as 1946, Richard Acland wrote in his *Public Speaking*:

> You need not to try to be an orator. You need not have a loud voice; you need not talk like a BBC announcer. There does not need to be any particular beauty in your voice; and if, by nature not by artifice, you always talk with a trace, or even more than a trace, of your local dialect, so much the better. There is only one thing which you do need to have, and that is sincerity.

This is true. We want you to be just you, not someone else. It reminds me of the advice attributed to Franklin D. Roosevelt (but not coined by him) to speakers: 'Be brief, be sincere, be seated.'

There has been an increasingly revelatory tone in parliamentary speeches, with MPs being prepared to talk about aspects of their private lives which would have been taboo a decade ago. For example, many MPs have been prepared to discuss their mental health in the Chamber in a way that would have been career-ending a few years ago.

In 2019, Rosie Duffield MP made a contribution to the debate on domestic abuse which earned her a rare, and forbidden, round of applause at the end. She begins discussing coercive control in the abstract, and slowly reveals (spoiler alert) that she is describing her own experiences. It is chilling stuff.

> So what is domestic violence or abuse, and where do we get our ideas about it from? Often we see the same images and stereotypes on TV: housing estates, working-class families, drunk men coming home from the pub, women surrounded by children, and a sequence of shouting, followed by immediate physical violence or assault. But soap opera scenes tend to focus on only one or two aspects of a much bigger and more complex picture.
>
> Domestic violence has many faces, and the faces of those who survive it are varied, too. There are 650 MPs in this place – 650 human beings. Statistically, it is highly likely that some of us here will have directly experienced an abusive relationship, and we are just as likely as anyone else to have grown up in a violent household.
>
> Abuse is not just about noticeable physical signs. Sometimes there are no bruises. Abuse is very often all about

control and power; it is about abusers making themselves feel big, or biggest, but that is not how they present themselves. It is not how they win your heart. It is not how they persuade you to meet them for a coffee, then go to a gig, and then spend an evening snuggled up in front of a movie at their place. When they ask you out, they do not present their rage and do not tell you that while they like the idea of strong, independent, successful women, they do not like the reality. They do not threaten, criticise, control, yell, or exert their physical strength in an increasingly frightening way – not yet. Not at the start. Not when they think you are sweet, funny and gorgeous. Not when they want to impress you. Not when they turn up to only your third date with chocolate, and then jewellery. Not when they meet your friends, your parents, or the leader of your political party. They do not do any of that then.

It is only later, when the door to your home is locked, that you really start to learn what power and control look and feel like. That is when you learn that 'I'll always look after you', 'I'll never let you go', and 'you're mine for life' can sound menacing and are used as a warning over and over again. It is when the ring is on your finger that the mask can start to slip, and the promises sound increasingly like threats. It is then that you spend twelve or more hours at work longing to see the person you love, only to find that on the walk or tube journey home they refuse to speak a single, solitary word to you. Eventually, at home, they will find a way to let you know which particular sin you have apparently committed: your dress was too short, the top you wore in the Chamber was too low-cut, or you did not respond to a message immediately.

It starts slowly: a few emotional knocks, alternated with romantic gushes and promises of everlasting love, which leave you reeling, confused, spinning around in an ever-changing but always hyper-alert state, not knowing what mood or message awaits you. You tell yourself to be less sensitive, less emotional, to stop over-analysing every little thing. Ignore the moods – he never stops saying he adores you, right? All seems good again.

A whole week goes by: a week of summer evening walks home and maybe a drink on the way. A long weekend is booked and organised as a surprise while you are at work. The journey there is full of promise and promises – time away alone together in a place away from stress – but then it starts. In a strange city, his face changes in a way you are starting to know and dread, in a way that says you need to stay calm, silent and very careful. He goes for a walk. You sit in your hotel room and wait. You read a city guide and plan which sights you want to visit, mentally packing a day full of fun. But he seems to have another agenda. He doesn't want you to leave the room. He has paid a lot of money and you need to pay him your full attention. You are expected to do as you are told, and you know for certain what that means – so you do exactly as you are told.

In the months that follow, those patterns continue: reward, punishment, promises of happily ever after alternated with abject rage, menace, silent treatment and coercive control; financial abuse and control; a point-blank refusal to disclose his salary or earnings, an assumption and insistence on it being okay to live in your home without contributing a single penny, as bills continue to pile up; a refusal to work, as your salary is great and public knowledge; false promises to start paying some specific bills, which you discover months later remain unpaid; and the slow but sure disappearance of any kindness, respect or loving behaviour.

You get to the stage where you are afraid to go home. After fifteen hours at work, you spend another hour on the phone to your mum or a close friend, trembling, a shadow of your usual self. You answer the phone, and the sheer nastiness and rage tell you not to go home at all. So you leave work with your best friend, exhausted and shaking, and buy a toothbrush on the way, knowing that the verbal abuse followed by silent refusal to speak at all will be 100 times worse tomorrow.

Every day is emotionally exhausting. You are working in a job you love but putting on a brave face and pretending all is good, fine – wonderful, in fact. Then the pretence and the public face start to drop completely: being yelled at in the car with the windows down, no attempt to hide behaviour during constituency engagements – humiliation and embarrassment now added to permanent trepidation and constant hurt and pain. It is impossible to comprehend that this is the person who tells his family how much he loves you and longs to make you his wife.

But the mask has slipped for good, and questions are starting. Excuses are given to worried friends, concerned family and colleagues who have started to notice. One night, after more crying and being constantly verbally abused because you suggest he pay a bit towards your new sofa, you realise you've reached the end and you simply cannot endure this for another day or week, and certainly not for the rest of your life. Having listened intently for two whole weeks to the sound of his morning shower, timing the routine until you know it off by heart, you summon up the courage to take his front-door keys from his bag.

You have tried everything else on earth and know for certain, 100 per cent, what awaits you that night if you do not act today. Heart banging, you hide them carefully and creep back into bed, praying he won't discover what you have done. You know for certain what will happen if he does. You know an apology will not follow. You know for sure it will be because of what you have done and that it is all your fault. He leaves for the gym, telling you how much he adores you. He tells you to remember that you will always be his. He kisses you lovingly, as though there has not been months of verbal abuse, threats and incidents he knows you will never disclose. He tells you he will bring something nice home for dinner.

Sure enough, the next few days and weeks are a total hell – texts and calls and yelling, 'You've locked me out like a

> dog,' 'No one treats me that way,' 'This is the last thing you will ever do.' You cry, you grieve for your destroyed dreams, you try to heal, you ignore the emails from wedding companies, but it is like withdrawal, and it takes six months.
>
> But one day you notice that you're smiling, that it's okay to laugh, and that it's been a week or two since the daily sobbing stopped. You realise you are allowed to be happy. You dare to relax and you dare to start to feel free. You realise it is not your fault and that he is now left alone with his rage and narcissism. You dare to start dating someone, and you realise that you have survived, but the brightest and most precious thing of all is realising that you are loved and believed by friends, family and colleagues who believe in you and support you.
>
> So if anyone is watching and needs a friend, please reach out, if it is safe to do so, and please talk to any of us, because we will be there and we will hold your hand. [Applause.]

This is a powerful speech because it is personal and relies on the slowly dawning realisation that the woman in the speech is Duffield herself. This is how to be authentic. A dry read-through of a policy brief would have little impact or power; instead, her story chills the blood.

The Speaker of the House responded once the applause had died down: 'I thank the hon. lady for that speech, which was simultaneously as horrifying and as moving a contribution in the Chamber as I have heard in my twenty-two years of membership of the House. Thank you.'

BUILD THE SPEECH WITH CONCRETE

As you write, try to avoid the abstract, the obscure, and the vague. We need concrete language, not abstractions and jargon. The simple test for your language is, can you see it? I can see a 'hospital', but I can't see a 'healthcare system'. I can see a 'flat', 'house' or 'home' but not 'affordable housing'.

An 'economy' is abstract. 'Jobs', 'factories', 'cash' and 'shops' are concrete.

The English language is the product of many influences: Latin, Greek, Norman French, Germanic languages, Anglo-Saxon, with a rich, and huge, vocabulary that reflects our history of invasion, empire, immigration and trade. This gives us lots of options, which is not always a positive thing. The best advice is to err towards the short, sharp Anglo-Saxon word rather than the flowery Latinate word (or its Norman French successor).

Better to 'take part' than 'participate'. Best to 'stop' or 'halt' rather than to 'terminate'. These words carry more meaning and sound better when said out loud in a speech. Churchill is said to have said, 'Broadly speaking, the short words are the best, and the old words best of all.'

If using a metaphor, the same applies. A good metaphor rests on an easily recognised image with concrete language. Here's Ben Howlett MP during a debate on tackling ISIS (or ISIL): 'One of my key concerns was that we cut off the head of the ISIL snake, only for it to grow up elsewhere.'

BUILDING A STRUCTURE

Once you have solid content for your speech, you need to give it an architecture. You need a structure. Unlike other forms of writing, a speech has a structure based on the attention span of the audience. A written document can be read, re-read, started on one day and finished on another, read in parts, or read in a different order than the way it was written. We can scan it or read it line by line. It can be supported by tables and charts, footnotes and appendices. There are clear headings, punctuation and designs to make it clear to the reader. A speech has none of these.

The way a speech is structured is different from a written document, and you can hear when someone tries to read out a policy brief in the Chamber as though it were a speech. If you've written essays, you'll know that an essay starts by setting out an argument, reviewing the evidence for and against and building to a brilliant conclusion. Ta-da! A speech is nothing like this.

At its most basic, a speech has a beginning, middle and end.

There are graphs that show how audiences are listening to the start of a speech, and their attention starts to wane in the middle, and then spikes at the end. This is certainly true for longer speeches delivered at conferences and seminars, and it has some validity for parliamentary speeches, even though they are shorter.

In the ancient world, Cicero, Quintilian and the rest of the rhetoricians put forward their differing views of how a speech should be structured. They agreed that *arrangement* was one part of rhetoric, but they did not agree on what exactly it should look like. This makes perfect sense, of course, especially when it comes to parliamentary speeches, which must fit the time limit, circumstance, and motive purpose.

One version of *arrangement* is this:

- *exordium*, or 'opening'
- *narration*, or 'statement of facts'
- *divisio* or *partitio*, that is, the statement of the point at issue and exposition of what the orator proposes to prove
- *confirmation*, or 'exposition of arguments'
- *confutatio,* or 'refutation of one's opponent's arguments'
- *conclusio,* or 'peroration'

A parliamentary speech should contain a clear *exordium* and *conclusio*, but the writer may decide whether to include a clear *confutatio* of their opponent's case, and how much time there is for multiple arguments and proof points. Classical orators did not have just four minutes to make their arguments.

A modern version is the PROVE model, which is drawn from classical rhetoric:

- Proposal for what you want to argue
- Reasons why the proposal is a good one
- Objections and other points of view
- Verification from trusted sources
- End with a solid finish

So if the speech is in favour of a statutory sauna in every workplace, you would use PROVE like this:

- Proposal: every workplace with over twenty employees must, by law, provide a free sauna for the workforce
- Reasons: the evidence suggests that this helps worker productivity, team-building and has demonstrable mental health benefits.
- Objections: it is profoundly un-British, might promote inappropriate behaviours and be intimidating for staff members, plus saunas are expensive and make you lazy
- Verification: the University of Helsinki's department for sauna studies shows that saunas prompt a 23 per cent increase in productivity; the Sauna Association has a survey of 100 workplaces with saunas which shows 87 per cent of staff appreciate the opportunity to use the facility in the office; the Department for Public Health has a study into the mental health benefits of saunas which shows 75 per cent of people using saunas reported better mental health
- End: far from being un-British, we are a nation of lidos and public baths, and the sauna builds on our tradition. We need people to return to the office. We need to tackle the mental health crisis. We need to increase productivity. Saunas are the answer

Golly, I'm even starting to persuade myself this is a good idea.

Whichever type of structure you adopt, from the simplest

to more complex, use clear headings and signposts to elide from one section to the next.

HOW TO START A PARLIAMENTARY SPEECH

It is a convention to praise the previous speaker, with some pertinent remark about them or what they've said. This is for the member to extemporise, because you won't know who the previous speaker is until they've spoken.

Here's the SNP MP Allan Dorans observing this nicety:

'It is always a pleasure to follow the right hon. Member for Ludlow…'

Or Diana Johnson MP doing the same:

'I pay tribute to the Chair of the Defence Committee, the right hon. Member for Horsham, for the speech he has just made. I agree with every word he said, and I thought he put it incredibly eloquently.'

Here's Will Quince MP:

'It is an honour to follow my hon. friend the Member for Hendon, who made a very powerful speech.'

The MP might need to draw the House's attention to the Register of Members' Financial Interests at the start of the speech. The register is there to make transparent 'any financial interest which a member has, or any benefit which he or she receives, which others might reasonably consider to influence his or her actions or words as a Member of Parliament'.

For example, if the debate is about employment law, and the member is sponsored by a trade union, or if the debate is on leasehold reform, and the member owns property, then they must declare their interest. The form of words here is usually, 'Let me begin by referring to my entries in the Register of Members' Financial Interests.'

Next, a speech should start by setting out the argument. You do this at the start to make it clear what the speech is about and establish the theme. A speech is not a crime novel, where we have to guess what's going on and only find out at the end. A speech should clearly start with a bargain with the audience – I'm going to talk about *this*. This is the *exordium* we mentioned earlier: the setting out of the case in classical rhetoric.

Here's Peter Luff MP in 2006, starting his adjournment debate speech on the deteriorating quality of the answers to Parliamentary Questions:

> My speech seeks to do three things. First, it will illustrate the worrying deterioration in the quality of answers given by ministers by drawing on my recent experience, although I know that other members have similar stories to tell. Secondly, it will express serious concern about members' tendency to ask unnecessarily large numbers of questions – that is certainly part of the explanation for the declining quality. Thirdly, it will offer three simple solutions to the volume problem, in the hope that ministers and departments will respond by offering more timely and helpful replies.

This is as clear as it gets. It sets up a clear structure, with numbered points, for the audience to follow. It creates a route to go down. It helps Peter Luff deliver his points in order, without forgetting anything or doing it in the wrong order. Luff probably learned at school that a sound structure for a speech is:

1. Tell them what you're going to tell them
2. Tell them
3. Tell them what you've told them

Forgive me if you've heard that before, but it remains one of the soundest structures for a speech. It creates anticipation. It reinforces the points by saying them three times. It is easier to remember. And if delivered well, it shows that the member has a logical, ordered mind, with a considered and thought-through speech and not just a jumble of random thoughts delivered on the hoof.

The reason given for not allowing 'reading' is to allow some cut and thrust in a debate. G. F. M. Campion, in his *An Introduction to the Procedures of the House of Commons* in 1929, says, 'The prohibition of the reading of speeches discourages rhetoric and puts a premium on the debater's talent of finding his points in the earlier speeches.' Note the pejorative use of 'rhetoric'. However, Campion's substantive point is correct. A successful speech should address some of the points made by previous speakers, which means paying attention and thinking about how to respond in the Chamber. It's also the reason why MPs should stay in the Chamber during debates to hear speeches, and not just grandstand.

HOW TO LAND A PARLIAMENTARY SPEECH

Conservative politician Lord Mancroft said, 'A speech is like a love affair: any fool can start one, but to end it requires considerable skill.' He wasn't wrong.

We tend to remember the first and last of things, for example lists, the start and ends of films or the first and last candidate in a job interview. With a speech, we usually recall the start and the end. The end section of a speech is called the peroration, and it should sum up the argument, repeat the key theme and 'land' the speech with a resounding final flourish. The MP must keep an eye on the timer and not run out of time. Nor should they rush through their final lines as the clock ticks down. The real skill is to switch to the end just in time.

In a debate, the member can finish by asking questions to the minister, because the minister must 'reply' to the debate by picking up all the points and questions made during the debate. If you are writing one of the final or 'winding up' speeches, you leave space for this summing-up of key contributions by other members. Hilary Benn MP's speech in 2015 on tackling ISIS is remembered as an important and powerful parliamentary speech. But look at the hoops he had to jump through before he got into his stride:

> We have heard a number of outstanding speeches. Sadly, time will prevent me from acknowledging them all. I would just like to single out the contributions, both for and against the motion, from my right hon. friends the Members for Derby South, for Kingston upon Hull West and Hessle, and

> for Normanton, Pontefract and Castleford; my hon. friends the Members for Barnsley Central, and for Wakefield; my right hon. friend the Member for Wolverhampton South East; my hon. friends the Members for Brent North, for Liverpool, West Derby, for Wirral West, for Stoke-on-Trent North and for Birmingham Ladywood; the hon. Members for Reigate, for South West Wiltshire, and for Tonbridge and Malling; the right hon. Member for Chichester; and the hon. Member for Wells.

The frontbencher winding up must take a note of every member speaking, their constituency and ideally a line or two of what they've said.

You should aim to end the speech on a stressed syllable, to give it some punch. I'm reminded of Giles Coren's infamous furious memo to the subs on *The Times* who had had the temerity to remove an 'a' from the last line of one of his reviews, which resulted in the final syllable being unstressed:

> When you're winding up a piece of prose, metre is crucial. Can't you hear? Can't you hear that it is wrong? It's not fucking rocket science. It's fucking pre-GCSE scansion. I have written 350 restaurant reviews for *The Times* and I have never ended on an unstressed syllable. Fuck. fuck, fuck, fuck.

One of Winston Churchill's most famous speeches was to members of this Cabinet on 28 May 1940. The speech cemented

Britain's policy of prosecuting the war with Hitler and banishing those who favoured appeasement. The end goes like this:

> I have thought carefully in these last few days whether it was part of my duty to consider entering negotiations with that man. [But if we did that,] we should become a slave state … I am convinced that every man of you would rise up and tear me down from my place if I were for one moment to contemplate parley or surrender. If this long island story of ours is to end, let it end only when each of us lies choking in his own blood upon the ground.

But wouldn't it have been better if Churchill had said, 'Let it end only when each of us lies upon the ground, choking in his own blood'? Blood is a stronger word than ground.

Here's Sir Jeremy Quin ending his speech in a defence debate in May 2024:

'We need to invest: in innovation, in capital equipment, and in the men and women in our armed forces. I am pleased that the government are doing just that. It is vital, it is timely, and every penny must be well spent.'

'Spent' is a stressed syllable. You should always try to end on a solid, concrete, single-syllable word like this.

THE NEED FOR ELASTICITY

One thing that keeps an MP on their toes when speaking, and gives the speechwriter a headache, is that the length of the speech may be shortened in the middle of the debate itself.

In other settings – a think tank seminar, village fete, or party conference – there is a set amount of minutes allocated to the speech, and it's always a good idea to undershoot. No one wants a long speech.*

If a member is going on too long, the Speaker will shut them up. Independent MP Jeremy Corbyn, in asking a question to the Prime Minister on the NATO and European Political Community Meetings statement in July 2024, started to make his single transferable speech about Israel. The Speaker closed him down: 'Order. May I say gently to the right hon Gentleman that I have a lot more to get in today, and as important as his message is, I need to make others heard?'

The timings of a speech are down to the Speaker or Deputy Speaker. If there are many MPs wanting to speak, the length of speeches may be limited to three minutes, as Sir Chris Bryant MP mentions in his magisterial two-volume history of Parliament:

> Often there are so many wishing to say their piece that the Speaker sets and enforces a strict time limit of between three and fifteen minutes (a 21st-century innovation); certainly two-hour addresses with elaborate rhetorical flourishes and lengthy classical allusions are a thing of the past, today's MPs preferring to raise matters of direct concern to their constituents as pithily as possible just before issuing a press release.

* I'm reminded of the MP speaking at their constituency meeting who misheard the chair's exhortation to keep it to 'four to five minutes' and spoke for forty-five minutes.

The imperative to issue a press release has probably been supplanted by the WhatsApp to the office 'post my speech on socials'. And certainly lengthy classical allusions are few and far between, but hey, *tempora mutantur, nos et mutamur in illis*, as Ovid never said.

The trick here is to build some elasticity into the speech, with sections that can be jettisoned, like the rockets on a spaceship, to allow the key sections to fly.

It might work like this:

- Section A (one minute) – the *exordium*, setting out the argument, after all the parliamentary protocols
- Section B (one minute) – key facts and figures supporting the argument, drawn from respected sources (the House of Commons Library, for example)
- Section C (one minute) – an anecdote to illustrate the key points
- Section D (one minute) – challenges to the government, or questions to the minister, or attacks on your opponents
- Section E (one minute) – summing up the argument with strong finish

If this five-minute speech has to become a three-minute speech, you can't just lop off the final two minutes. Instead, you can lose the anecdote in Section C and shave a few seconds from Section B and Section D. The speechwriter can help by clearly marking sections on the speaker's note or bullet points and agreeing in advance what can be jettisoned. You could mark these with brackets, or a different font, or a different colour.

BUILDING IN THE SOCIAL MEDIA CLIP

On 20 April 2022, Sir Keir Starmer shot the following quip at the Prime Minister: 'Yesterday's apology lasted for as long as the Prime Minister thought necessary to be clipped for the news.' He was describing the age-old practice of using a phrase designed for the media. We used to call this a 'soundbite' for the broadcasters. Since the advent of social media, the clip is not only for the television and radio but also for Facebook, TikTok and X.

If you want to know how to master the social media clip, look no further than Donald Trump. His speeches are atrocious. They ramble on without form or function. What his team have realised is that structure doesn't matter, as long as there's a clip for Fox News and social media platforms. A twenty-second clip can be viewed by hundreds of millions of people within hours. Consider his greatest hits: 'Drain the swamp,' 'Lock her up,' 'Make America great again,' 'Build the wall.' Or Trump's press conference after being found guilty of a felony. He rambled on, but the ringing phrase was that the judge looked like an angel but was in reality the devil. The fact that these soundbites are in your mind, like an annoying earworm, is testament to their repetition across social media.

You need to write a social media clip into the speech and make it clear in advance which bit is designed to be clipped and put on your Facebook page, X, Threads and so on. There's no point trying to decide afterwards which bit was good. You should know beforehand. Then the parliamentary team can use the parliamentary TV website to download a clip and bung it up on your socials; the faster the better.

The media may be new and evolving fast, but the concept is not. Speechwriters have always tried to get a ringing phrase into a speech, one that defines it, frames the argument and gets onto the evening news. One of the most notorious speeches of the post-war period is Enoch Powell's 'Rivers of Blood' speech in 1968.

It is a deeply unpleasant affair, packed to the gunnels with racist imagery. The key phrase that gives it its title comes from Powell, a classicist, using an allusion to Virgil's *Aeneid*. But despite the presence of an ATV camera crew, the key phrase is unrecorded because the camera operators popped out for a fag. If you have a soundbite, make sure you tell broadcasters beforehand.

SIGNPOSTING YOUR SPEECH

Imagine for a moment I invited you on a walking tour around Westminster. We would meet outside the Red Lion at midday and be joined by a professional tour guide. Assuming you were free, and you turned up, what would you ask the guide? Probably two things. One, where are we going? Two, what are we going to see? These are reasonable questions. But what if the tour guide refused to answer them and insisted that we should just follow? Would you go? Would you go for a few minutes out of curiosity? Or would you turn back after a while, disappointed and frustrated?

Now, what is true of a tight-lipped tour guide is also true of a parliamentarian who gives little or no clue about where we are heading in the speech, what the main things are to listen out for, how long it will take and when we are nearly there. A speaker who just starts speaking without signposts is maddening, and the audience will swiftly switch off.

You need to write signposts into the speech, to guide the listener, to give structure and form, and to ensure the speaker doesn't stray from the path. There is little worse than an MP who heads down every rabbit hole and wanders off down every dead-end.

What are signposts? They are phrases that guide the listener through the speech. They include phrases such as:

- I've three points I'd like to make this afternoon
- That was my second point, and my third point is this…
- There's one thing that matters more than anything
- To conclude my remarks, let me say…

On that last one, if you signpost that you are about to finish the speech, you must finish it. There is nothing worse than a speaker who signals a close is coming, then carries on regardless.

There are broadly three kinds of signposts. There are those that tell us where we are, those that tell us where we are going and those that tell us that something important is coming up.

For the speechwriter, it is important to go over your draft and insert signposts, as they do not flow naturally into the first draft. You need to take a mallet and hammer them in, very consciously and deliberately, or else they may be missed out.

You might choose to use numbers to separate your key points, like this: 'I have three points I want to make this afternoon, Madam Deputy Speaker, and my first is…'

In rhetoric, this device is called *enumeratio*, or using numbers to count out your main points or arguments.

Here's Margaret Thatcher, as Leader of the Opposition, in the no-confidence debate in 1979. She makes her arguments about the state having too much control, the unions too much power and so on, but she divides her speech up into four parts, using *enumeratio*. To guide the House, she uses these linking phrases:

- 'There are, I believe, four main things that have contributed to Britain's decline in the last five years'
- 'That, I believe, is the first reason for the decline'
- 'The second reason for the decline is…'
- 'The third reason for our problems is…'
- 'The fourth reason for our decline…'
- 'There we have the record and some of the reasons for failure'

And in doing so, she gives herself a clear architecture and the House a guide to what is going on. This approach serves to not only help the audience, but also the speaker, to follow the argument in a sequential way. Like all signposts, it helps us to avoid getting lost.

Here's Aneurin Bevan in 1942, attacking the wartime coalition: 'First, the main strategy of the war has been wrong; second, the wrong weapons have been produced; and third, those weapons are being managed by men who are not trained in the use of them and who have not studied the use of modern weapons.'

The numbers give the listener a clear sense of how the speaker is marshalling his material.

There is little worse than a speech that appears to be a stream of consciousness. This is a literary technique that reveals the disordered, disjointed and unpunctuated inner monologue of the character. Think James Joyce's *Ulysses* or Virginia Woolf's *Mrs Dalloway*. While stream of consciousness is a marvellous way to show inner turmoil and the plight of the modern soul, it is a terrible way to make a persuasive and compelling speech.

A speech needs order, structure, flow, and sequence. Like a building, a speech needs an architecture with sound foundations, storeys, and a roof. It needs to stand up as well as stand out. Clear signposts and headings give the listener a fighting chance of understanding what the speaker is trying to say and help the speaker deliver the speech in a logical, ordered manner without missing bits out or straying off-piste.

CHAPTER THREE

WHAT KIND OF SPEECH?

So, you're sitting in your office in Norman Shaw or Portcullis House. It's almost certainly cramped and overcrowded with staff. Since I first worked there in 1991, I have never seen a tidy parliamentary office. Some businesses have a 'clean-desk' policy. Parliamentary offices have the opposite: a 'pile-it-up-on-the-desk-floor-and-shelves' policy. Briefings and papers are piled high. Awards from lobbying groups are placed on shelves. Reminders of your constituency adorn the walls: pictures drawn by local school children, thank-you cards from residents, and so on.

You are contemplating writing a speech. You may have some brilliant ideas, big themes, passionate points you want to make. You want to leave a mark and give a voice to your constituents. You want to be noticed by the whips, perched on the front bench taking notes of which MPs speak well, show promise and, above all, display loyalty to the party leadership.

To start with, you need to be clear what kind of speech you are delivering. Parliament has evolved over centuries and there are different speech types designed for different purposes. A good parliamentarian needs to understand the differences and the need to vary the tone and content accordingly. If you are a staffer or parliamentarian, the Whips' Office, your parliamentary party office and your colleagues are three places to check what is required. And the House authorities themselves, including the Speaker's Office, remain the best source of advice.

If the MP's conversation with their researcher runs along the lines of 'I'd like to speak in the education debate on Wednesday – can you draft me some bullet points. Something about school cuts. Or perhaps language provision? Or maybe school meals. And say something nice about St Cuthbert's,' the result may well be a disaster. You need clarity of purpose, a clear commission to the writer and time cleared in the diary to make it happen.

Winston Churchill once described a fellow parliamentarian as follows: 'He can best be described as one of those orators who, before they get up, do not know what they are going to say; when they are speaking, do not know what they are saying; and, when they have sat down, do not know what they have said.'

You do not want to be one of those.

An early and important step is to establish what kind of parliamentary speech you aim to write and deliver.

DIFFERENT KINDS OF PARLIAMENTARY SPEECH

Parliament has two broad functions under our arcane, uncodified, yet robust, constitution. The first is to make the laws of the land. The second is to hold the government to account.

There is a third, somewhat nebulous function, which is to represent the nation.

Lawmaking involves a series of parliamentary stages that turn ideas into laws, where MPs make speeches. The scrutiny function is conducted via the select committee system, via oral and written Parliamentary Questions (including Prime Minister's Questions on a Wednesday) and through the speeches MPs make. The third function, speaking for the nation, is conducted through a variety of occasions, such as debates on big moments like the death of a monarch. In each of these, parliamentarians make speeches with different conventions, different timings and for different reasons.

MAIDEN SPEECH

This is the first speech a parliamentarian will make. The term 'maiden' is used in the same way as a 'maiden voyage' of a ship, or a 'maiden over' in cricket, to mean untouched, unmarried or even virginal. This patriarchal and outmoded etymology prompted the Australian Parliament to drop the use of 'maiden' and replace it with 'first', and I imagine the Westminster Parliament will eventually go the same way, but not before a row about wokery and political-correctness-gone-mad.

Some MPs wait for months before delivering their Maiden Speech, some even a year. Some think the best advice is to get it over with as soon as possible, like having a tooth extracted, and get on with the job of representing your constituents. Alternatively, you can wait your turn and spend time getting it right.

Until you've got the whole ghastly business over and done with, you cannot, as an MP, speak in any debate, speak on a ten-minute rule bill or move an amendment to a bill or motion. However, before your Maiden Speech, you can ask Parliamentary Questions, table written questions, take part in committees, present a Private Members' Bill and present a petition. You can even intervene in another member's speech and get yourself into Hansard before making a speech yourself.

If you're delivering a Maiden Speech, or writing one, you may find it a nerve-wracking affair. Margaret Hodge recalls:

> I was absolutely petrified that I was going to stutter, but I got through it. My husband and four children were here watching me. I did the usual thing of sitting down and listening to a couple of speeches then we all went to have a cup of tea and some scones. I came back for the wind-ups and sat in the corner. Suddenly, I heard the mighty voice of Betty Boothroyd admonishing me for having sat in the wrong place, because I did not have a clue that the protocols of the House meant that we had to sit where we had given our speech, when we came back for the wind-ups.

The wind-ups, by the way, are the closing speeches in a debate, not jibes designed to make MPs angry.

The debate on the King's Speech, which normally lasts six days at the start of a parliament, is a great opportunity to make your Maiden Speech. About ten new members can speak on each day. If you don't get in then (and everyone will be trying to), you have to wait for another debate. The Order Paper will alert you to opportunities.

The speech needs to relate in some way to the subject of the debate. If your MP is lucky to be speaking on one of the six days during the debate on the King's Speech, there will be a broad topic under discussion. You can find a cause or issue based on your MP's own interests and passions. If your MP speaks later in the parliament, or after a by-election, you need to link the speech to the motion being debated.

You must offer praise to the previous Member of Parliament. You may find yourself having to write praise for an MP you have just defeated in the election or one who has resigned in disgrace and prompted a by-election. No matter the enmity between the new MP and the previous one, you have to find something nice to say about them, and your MP has to grit their teeth and say it out loud. It's a test of character.

For example, Labour's Olivia Blake, MP for Sheffield Hallam, had the unenviable task of finding something nice to say about Jared O'Mara, her predecessor. O'Mara, dubbed the 'first Momentum MP', has the following headings on his Wikipedia page:

'Labour whip suspension over online comments'

'Reinstatement and resignation from Labour Party'

'Sexual harassment allegation'

'Allegations of corruption'

'Standing down'

'Criminal prosecution'

So as you can imagine, O'Mara's brief parliamentary career was less than glittering. He never asked an oral question and rarely spoke. Here's what his successor, Olivia Blake, said about him:

> It is traditional for newly elected MPs to thank their predecessors upon entering the Commons. Jared O'Mara, the previous MP for Sheffield Hallam, highlighted important issues relating to the accessibility of this House. For that, he should be commended. While he had his faults, many of which he himself admits, I note that members have recalled that his intervention in Westminster Hall on his own experience of autism was moving and brought the issue up the agenda.

And with that, she moved swiftly on.

Next, you need to say something about your constituency, its notable features, history and people. For example, in his Maiden Speech, Labour's Stephen Kinnock said of his constituency Aberavon in South Wales:

> It is truly an honour to be representing the constituency of Aberavon, where we are surrounded by the stirring spectacle of the Upper Afan Valley and the gentler rural beauty of Margam and Skewen. Looking out from our magnificent Aberavon beach, we survey the Celtic Sea and, further, the Atlantic Ocean, the symbol of my constituency's long, proud and productive engagement with global trade and industry.

He makes it sound every bit as beautiful as I am sure it is. He goes on to name-check some famous sons, with a clever segue:

> It is hardly surprising that Aberavonites have drama in their blood when one considers the drama of the landscape in which they are born. Anthony Hopkins and Michael Sheen are just two of the local lads made good, but perhaps the most famous of Aberavon's sons is Richard Burton, who is said to have mused that 'the Welsh are all actors, it's only the bad ones who become professional'. I am of course relieved to say he is not on record as having said the same thing about the Welsh and politicians.

Or here's American-born Joy Morrissey, Conservative MP for Beaconsfield, in her Maiden Speech on 24 February 2020 (two months after being elected):

> I will be working for the good of everyone, but I will of course be working for the good of Beaconsfield just a little bit more. With its amazing towns and villages, who could ask for more? It showcases all aspects of British life, whether it is the picturesque market towns of Marlow and Beaconsfield; or the historic villages that date back to the Domesday Book, like Taplow, Denham, Hedgerley and Burnham; or the Iron Age hill fort in Gerrards Cross; or the rich history of the three – count them, three – distinct villages within the Ivers.
>
> Beaconsfield has been home to influential thinkers, artists and entrepreneurs of the day, from William Penn,

> the founder of Pennsylvania – I thought we would do an American theme today; why not? – whose estate sits within picturesque Stoke Poges; to Barry Gibb, lead singer of the Bee Gees; to Pinewood Studios, a global leader in the creative arts.

You can see it follows the same pattern – praise for place, then notable people. If you want to study these in further detail, the House of Commons Library can provide constituency profiles, as well as the Maiden Speeches by previous MPs in that seat.

The convention is for the speech to be 'non-controversial', which means it steers clear of party political attacks or jibes. Most manage this – there is plenty of time for the rough and tumble. A few MPs seek to flout the convention by sticking the boot in, to show how committed and uncompromising they are. This mostly works in the opposite way, making them look a bit silly. Laura Pidcock, the Corbynite MP for North West Durham, used her Maiden Speech in June 2017 to excoriate Parliament, the establishment and capitalism. She got many thousands of social media 'hits'. She then lost the seat, which had had a Labour majority of nearly 9,000, to the Conservatives in December 2019.

In 1952, Aneurin Bevan, the Welsh Labour MP and architect of the NHS, described what happens when the new MP gets the tone all wrong in his or her maiden:

> It is when he learns that passionate feeling must never find expression in forthright speech. His first speech teaches him

> that. Having come straight from contact with his constituents, he is full of their grievances and his own resentment, and naturally, he does his best to shock his listeners into some realisation of it. He delivers himself therefore with great force and, he hopes and fears, with considerable provocativeness. When his opponent arises to reply he expects to hear an equally strong and uncompromising answer. His opponent does nothing of the sort. In strict conformity with parliamentary tradition, he congratulates the new member upon a successive Maiden Speech and expresses the urbane hope that the House will have frequent opportunities of hearing him in the future. The members present endorse this quite insincere sentiment with murmurs of approval. With that, his opponent pays no more attention to him, but goes on to deliver the speech he had intended to make. After remaining in his seat a little longer, the new member crawls out of the House with feelings of deep relief at having got it over, mingled with a paralysing sense of frustration. The stone he thought he had thrown turned out to be a sponge.

There are very few stones and plenty of sponges.

Barbara Castle recalls her Maiden Speech:

> I decided to slip it in unobtrusively at the quietest moment of the parliamentary week: 4 p.m. adjournment debate on a Friday afternoon … there were only two other MPs in the House, plus the amiable Minister of Labour, George Isaacs. The press gallery was apparently empty so I let fly, quoting

> a letter from a constituent who complained that as a skilled bricklayer he would be better employed building houses at home than 'acting as a grease-monkey to worn-out army lorries for a few hours each week'. The next morning I learned my first lessons in the art of parliamentary politics: never be deceived by an empty press gallery, and remember that a vivid phrase will get you anywhere. The word 'grease-monkey' had obviously caught the news editors' eyes and I was prominently reported in almost every newspaper.

There is much wisdom in Barbara Castle's identification of the importance of the 'vivid phrase'. A well-turned phrase can make your Maiden Speech (or any speech) stand out and grab some attention, especially in the modern age of social media.

The trick here is to consider a phrase that is short, telling and well-constructed. Social media likes sentences that are pithy and caustic. This is not the medium for drawn-out argument but for a phrase that pays. This is the realm of the zinger. Tech-savvy MPs stand in parts of the Chamber where their faces are unobstructed by the hanging microphones. They know that their words can be transmitted directly via their Facebook, X or TikTok to their constituents and beyond. For example, if you were Coventry MP Zarah Sultana, would you concern yourself with a fifteen-second clip on local BBC Radio Coventry and Warwickshire, with its 64,000 listeners, or speak directly to your half a million followers on TikTok? (The answer, actually, is probably both, as the demographics are so different.)

The very last Maiden Speech delivered in the Parliament elected in 2019 was by Chris Webb MP, elected in a by-election for Blackpool South on 2 May 2024, and delivered twenty-two days later in the final hours of the parliament. When the people of Blackpool sent Chris Webb to represent them, I doubt many were overly concerned with the Sanctions (EU Exit) (Miscellaneous Amendments and Revocations) Regulations 2024 (SI, 2024, No. 643), yet this is the debate into which he managed to slot his Maiden Speech, just before it was too late.

It serves as a useful template for how to do a Maiden Speech. Here it is, complete with my running commentary in brackets:

> Thank you, Mr Speaker.
>
> When it was announced that I was the winner of the Blackpool South by-election at 5:15 a.m. on 3 May, I called on the Prime Minister to hold a general election and give the rest of the country the same chance that my constituents had to vote for change and elect a new Labour government. I thank the Prime Minister for taking me up on that, although I had not expected to be back out on the campaign trail quite so soon. [A little light humour can get the Chamber onside.]
>
> I ask the whole House to join me in showing solidarity with my amazing – and now long-suffering – wife Portia, who has been at my side throughout with our amazing three-month-old son Cillian, who has brought so much joy

and laughter to our lives. [He's a family man and he loves his wife and kids.]

Mr Speaker, I am grateful for this opportunity to stand before you, at short notice. [It is always a good idea to suck up to the Speaker, and the reverse is also true: annoying the Speaker may see you not called to speak for months.]

It was the last opportunity to do so before a general election; had I not taken it, I risked a lifetime of being an answer to an obscure pub quiz question. [Chris Webb narrowly misses being the answer to the question, 'Which MPs never gave a speech?']

I relish getting back on the doorsteps and speaking with fellow residents.

I thank my predecessor, Scott Benton, and his staff for all their work and support of local residents. [You're supposed to wax lyrical about your predecessor. Perhaps here Chris Webb could have added a couple of sentences of praise about Scott Benton's hard work, but a quick look at his record tells us why he chose not to.]

I also thank Gordon Marsden for his personal support and tireless work in Blackpool South during his twenty-two years of service. Gordon is still fondly remembered and recognised for his huge contribution to my constituency and his pursuit of everyone having access to lifelong learning.

I would not be here today without two teachers who inspired and supported me as a young student with undiagnosed dyslexia. They helped me get to Hull University and on the road to this Chamber. Stephen Conway and Ken

Winstanley, I thank you. I would also like to pay special tribute to Anne Hoyer, a Labour giant on the Fylde coast whom we sadly lost last week. [You can use name-checks in your Maiden Speech: mentors, teachers, friends and family.]

[Here comes the history bit.] The first Blackpool constituency was created in 1885, a decade after the opening of the railway began to bring an influx of visitors to our town. In 1945, a separate Blackpool South constituency was created; it became clear that it had an identity of its own. It is home to the famous Pleasure Beach, Blackpool Tower and three piers. It has beaches with golden sands and, locals would argue, the best ice cream to be found anywhere at Notarianni's, which has served tourists and locals since 1928.

[And now the family story.] I am a child of tourism, my mum having moved to Blackpool to become a Redcoat in the '80s, but I am also a child of public service. My dad was a Blackpool postie who wanted to help and support fellow workers in Royal Mail, and then those in BT and others throughout the Communication Workers Union. Thanks to the last Labour government, my mum was able to retrain for free and became an early-years teaching assistant at my primary school – her dream job. Before them, there was my paternal nan, Val Harman, a scout leader who dedicated her life to inspiring young people; my paternal grandfather, Brian Harman, who was a local independent councillor and who, at eighty-three years old, is still heavily involved in his local community centre in Burntwood; and my paternal grandfather, Dougie Webb, who served in World

War Two, fighting fascism in Europe and Africa, and who once guarded Winston Churchill at Chequers – all of them public servants.

While I was tracing my paternal grandmother's history, I was amazed to find out how deep my family's public service roots go. I discovered that my fourteenth great-grandfather, Edmund Moody, saved the life of Henry VIII. The king, out hunting with his hawk, tried to reach over a ditch with a pole, which broke. Edmund, a footman of the king's, leapt into the water and saved him from drowning. Sadly, the £6-a-year pension and the land that he received as a reward did not stretch far enough to help his descendant, my nan Margaret Webb, who had a tough life growing up in Liverpool. I was raised not on stories of brave footmen who saved kings but on the stories of my nan and her sisters, who wore newspapers for shoes and battled TB during wartime without an NHS.

Through grit, determination and the welfare reforms of a progressive Labour government, my nan and granddad were able to move into one of the first council houses built in Blackpool in the '50s, in Grange Park. She went on to run a small business in Blackpool's famous Abingdon Street market. Having grown up without proper healthcare, she knew the value of our NHS and how vital it is that we protect it. I will make it my mission in this place to do so in her memory.

[Now we're back in Blackpool.] Since the pandemic, Blackpool has seen record numbers of visitors rightly returning to our beloved seaside town, which has so much to offer, but while tourism recovery is central to our town's future, it is time to focus on the recovery of our communities beyond the prom. After years of austerity, and now during the cost-of-living crisis, all too often, the town that I am proud to call home is recognised as being at the sharp end of statistics for poverty, crime, mental ill health, low life expectancy and more. I will work tirelessly for those communities – hopefully in the next parliament, too – and I hope to prove that politics has the power to change people's lives.

My heartfelt thanks go out to the people of Blackpool South, who put their trust in me on 2 May and elected me as their Blackpool-born-and-bred Member of Parliament. My hometown's motto is 'Progress'. The town that pioneered municipal street lighting, electric tramways and modern tourism for the working classes has continued to forge ahead, even with deep spending cuts. Blackpool South now has a Labour MP. Under what I hope is an imminent Labour government, I will fight to make sure that progress is possible for everyone in Blackpool, inspiring the next generation.

With economic stability, families in Blackpool South, where a third of children live in poverty, will not have to choose between heating and eating. Cuts to NHS waiting times will mean that those in Blackpool South, where people are twice as likely to die from heart disease by the age of seventy-five as people in wealthy areas, will be able to see a doctor when they need to. Hundreds more police on the streets will mean that in Blackpool, where weapon and knife offences have increased by more than 400 per cent since 2015, safety will be restored to our communities. [The House of Commons Library can supply these kinds of local facts and figures.]

But those painful statistics tell only half the story. Anyone from Blackpool will tell you to look behind the headlines and beyond the bright lights of the illuminations to find the real story of our town. It is alive with grassroots creativity and culture, has a thriving LGBTQ+ community and a wealth of fascinating lives that could only have been lived in Blackpool. It is a story of community resilience and of people who, with very little themselves, are always willing to give to someone else who has less. We have a wealth of community organisations and charities working hard to improve lives in Blackpool South. For their dedication to the town, I would like to thank Counselling in the Community and its inspirational founder, Stuart Hutton-Brown; Blackpool Food Bank; Fylde Coast Women's Aid; Reclaim Blackpool; Skool of Street; Blackpool Street Angels; Boathouse Youth; the Friends of Stanley Park; the St Peter's Church soup kitchen; and many others too numerous to mention. [This a clever bit of politics – naming various local groups and charities, so he can send them copies of Hansard afterwards, showing their name in lights.]

In closing, I would not be standing here today without the support of our good friend and my mentor, Tony Lloyd.

> Tony was an incredible northern Labour parliamentarian whom we sadly lost at the start of this year. 'For me, politics is all about people,' Tony once told me. 'It's that sense of human solidarity that matters. If it's not about making people's lives better, don't be a politician.' I am sad that he is not here to see me take my seat, but I will honour Tony's memory by serving my constituents in the same way that he served his: with people at the heart of my politics. [This is a solid way to end, by praising a respected and much-loved parliamentarian.]

The convention is that a Maiden Speech is not interrupted by interventions, and the next MP to speak must praise the MP's Maiden Speech, no matter how prosaic, mundane or not-very-good it is, as though it was like listening to Cicero address the senate.

Chris Webb's Maiden Speech provides a useful template. It makes much of the occasion, including the circumstances of his election and the late point in the parliament the speech is being delivered. He mixes the personal, the place and the political. He follows the conventions and does not try to 'make a name' for himself with some caustic attack on the Tories. Note too that his speech, as a maiden, has nothing whatsoever to do with the bill actually being debated. This is one time you can be completely off-topic without falling foul of SO42.

Here's Josh Babarinde, the new Liberal Democrat MP for Eastbourne, delivering his Maiden Speech in July 2024 (with commentary):

It was inspirational to listen to the story of the hon. Member for Bassetlaw [Jo White] and her determination to never stop dreaming. [He starts with an extemporised reference to the previous speech by Jo White MP. It is always better to pick up something from the debate and refer to it rather than merely reading from a prepared script.] It was also inspirational and fantastic to hear Maiden Speeches from many others. I was interested to hear the competition among some members about the length of piers in seaside towns. I hail from the great town of Eastbourne. While some hon. members might have a longer pier than mine, it is important to remember that what you do with it is most important. [This smutty joke probably belongs at the end of the pier, not Parliament.] On our pier we have cafes, we have bars and we have a former nightclub, at which I once organised parties. We have got it all going on on Eastbourne pier.

But it is also an inspiration, looking around this House and reading about its members, to see and be part of the most diverse parliament ever: more women than ever before; more LGBT people than ever before; and more Joshes than ever before – this House's population of Joshes went from zero to seven overnight on 4 July. That is what we call an open-door policy. If members struggle to remember which Josh I am, I can make it very simple for them: this Josh represents Eastbourne, officially the sunniest town in the UK. As an Eastbourne lad born and bred, it is the honour of my life to represent my home town and in particular to fight to protect services at our local hospital where I was born, the Eastbourne District General Hospital, as our Member of Parliament. I am so grateful to the people of Eastbourne for placing their trust in me.

Gorgeous sunrays aside, my town shines brightly in the many other accolades that it holds too [a neat metaphor]. We are the home of the first roller-skating ice rink in the UK in 1875, the first five-a-side football tournament in 1957 and the birthplace of the Arctic roll in 1958 [things in threes always sound better]. Most personally, Eastbourne is the town that made me.

Home was not always safe when I was growing up, but thanks to a wonderful family who loved me, thanks to Scout leaders at 1st Seaside Troop who challenged me, and thanks to teachers at Cavendish School who believed in me, Eastbourne gave me opportunity. In fact, there is a particular supply teacher I had who I want to pay tribute to right now: Caroline Ansell, who went on to become the Conservative MP for Eastbourne and is my predecessor. Mrs Ansell and I first met in the religious education classroom – Room 116 in Cavendish School – when I was fifteen years old. Perhaps she would have given me a detention or two had she known at that time that one day I would come for her next job at the ballot box some years later. But seriously, Caroline dedicated herself to Eastbourne, and I put my recognition of her commitment on the record.

I also pay tribute to another predecessor: Stephen Lloyd, my good friend, whose service to our town inspires my own. He is a complete and utter legend. There is another predecessor as the Member of Parliament for Eastbourne whose memory this House can, and must, never forget: Ian Gow, who served from 1974 until he was appallingly assassinated in 1990. A few years before my time, Ian Gow is remembered and still admired by Eastbournians as an extremely hard-working Member of Parliament. The shield that honours him in this House serves as a reminder of his service, his grave sacrifice and our duty to pursue debate and disagreement with civility, respect and peace. [This is a well-judged and fitting mention for Conservative MP Ian Gow, killed by the IRA.]

Turning to the subject of this debate, I want to share a migration story that says a lot about the character of my town. It started on a summer's day in 1960s Eastbourne, when a sweet, retired lady, Mrs Baker, noticed a curious sight. She saw another lady, also white, pushing a small black boy in a pram. Mrs Baker, curious, struck up a conversation with that woman and asked what was going on. Mrs Baker learned that the boy had been sent to live with that woman by a young Nigerian couple, and she was caring for the boy while the couple studied in London. Inspired, Mrs Baker said that she would love to do the same. Coincidentally, the black boy's mother was pregnant again, and was for a third time a couple of years later. Babies two and three were sent to live with the Baker family in Eastbourne. They were Toki Babarinde and Wale Babarinde, my uncle and my dad, and it was part of a sort of private fostering arrangement that was not uncommon between west African families and white families at that time, although it was not without its complications.

In my dad's case, and for his brothers too, moving to Eastbourne was a ticket to opportunity. They loved their upbringing, and Eastbourne embraced them. Sadly, my uncle Toki died earlier this year. Sat in the chapel during his funeral, I turned behind me, and among a sea of Nigerian faces was one white lady also paying her respects: Charmaine Baker from the Baker family. That moment gave me goosebumps, just like those moments when old-school Eastbournians look at me in all my brownness, all my gayness and all my working-class-rootedness and say, 'Josh, you are one of our own.'

I share that story to say that while Eastbourne's hospitality traditions are often associated with the mighty bucket and spade, they go far deeper. Eastbourne's true hospitality traditions are of generosity, welcome, tolerance, multiculturalism and compassion. The story of how I ended up in this House is testament to that, and I believe that with those values the same goes for our country, regardless of what other members in various places in this House may say.

While our town benefits from more sunshine hours than any other in the country, that blaring sun sometimes casts shadows, too. I am gutted to say that Eastbourne is also home to the busiest food bank in the country. Last year, it distributed more food parcels per head than any other food bank in the UK, according to the Trussell Trust. That is why, working with Eastbourne Foodbank's inspirational CEO, Howard Wardle, I led Eastbourne to become the first council in the country to declare a cost-of-living emergency and to unlock emergency funding for those struggling most. It is also why I sincerely believe that the government should be even more ambitious in leading the fight against poverty by scrapping the two-child benefit cap.

A compassionate state is by no means a state that makes us soft or weak. In fact, care is power. We cannot have enterprise, innovation or justice if we do not have a culture of care and compassion. That has underpinned my career's work, founding and running an organisation supporting vulnerable young people out of crime, out of gangs and into employment.

Our constituents have sent us here to be bold in rebuilding and reimagining our great country's spirit of having one another's backs. As Eastbourne's MP, I will strive to achieve nothing less.

Josh Babarinde's speech speaks warmly about his constituency, is peppered with personal anecdotes and fun facts, is deferential to his predecessors from whichever political party and has a little political grit towards the end. It has the important ingredient of self-effacement and humility, which serves a Maiden Speech well.

Maiden Speech checklist

- Get on with it. Don't leave it too late

- You need to alert the Speaker's Office that you want to make a Maiden Speech
- Decide which part of the parliamentary agenda you want to speak in
- Be uncontroversial
- Stick to the formula: praise for your predecessor, say something nice about your family, mentors, previous MPs, and your constituents
- Talk about the constituency, its history, landmarks, and notable residents
- The House of Commons Library will give you copies of previous members' Maiden Speeches, plus up-to-date constituency facts and figures
- Keep it brief and get it over with
- You can request a special bound copy of Hansard with your speech as a memento

SPEAKING IN DEBATES

There are different kinds of debates. Some are held in the Chamber, some in the Grand Committee Room, Westminster Hall. Of course, the House of Lords has its own debates, which have their own courtesies and conventions. There are Estimates Days, when the Commons spend three days on public expenditure. There are Second Reading debates, when bills are voted on. There are occasions when the Chamber is packed and others when it is almost deserted.

Before writing a speech for the Chamber, you need to maximise your chances of being called by the Speaker. In

Parliament, that's called catching the Speaker's eye. The best way to catch his or her eye is to email the Speaker's office in advance, and you will probably be called early. This is for Second or Third Readings of bills but not for a committee of the whole House, the report stage of a bill or to consider Lords amendments to bills. There's more than a courtesy here. It allows the Speaker to work out the length of speeches once the debate starts. That's why if the member can't turn up, they should alert the Speaker so they can recalibrate the timings.

Once you've put your name in, you need to turn up and stay in your seat for the debate. You won't be called if you miss the opening speeches and the next two. You'll be punished by not being called, perhaps for weeks afterwards.

There are time limits on speeches, and this may change during the debate as whoever is in the Chair decides. This means your five-minute speech may suddenly become a three-minute speech. We looked in the previous chapter at how to handle this elasticity. Even without a time limit, an MP should try to be focused and concise. The *Rules of Behaviour* guide for MPs says that 'you speak with reasonable brevity and be mindful of others', which is good advice.

Indeed, as the Conservative politician Lord Brabazon of Tara remarked, 'If you cannot say what you have to say in twenty minutes, you should go away and write a book about it.'

Parliamentary speeches used to be much longer. Some would last an hour or two. In 1853, Gladstone delivered the lengthiest budget speech on record, clocking in at four hours forty minutes while apparently drinking a mixture of egg and sherry. Those days, thankfully, are long gone. Disraeli, by contrast, delivered his 1867 Budget speech in just forty-five minutes. A lasting tradition is that the Chancellor may drink alcohol at the despatch box to help them get through it. Kenneth Clarke drank a tumbler of whisky, Geoffrey Howe had a gin and tonic, Nigel Lawson a spritzer, but Gordon Brown, Alistair Darling and George Osborne had only water.

THE GRACIOUS SPEECH

This is one speech which you are very unlikely to have a hand in as a speechwriter, unless you end up working at No. 10 for a Prime Minister. And as an MP, you will never give it. The Gracious Speech, more generally known as the King's Speech, is the moment when the government's political priorities are laid bare. It comprises a list of bills that MPs will soon be able to get their teeth into.

This speech is delivered by the monarch from the throne in the House of Lords at the State Opening of Parliament, with all the Ruritanian flummery that the British establishment can muster. Diamond tiaras, ermine cloaks, Yeoman of the Guard, the imperial crown – the full works. The speech is usually heard in respectful silence. In 1998, the Queen's Speech included a reference to abolishing most of the hereditary peers from the House of Lords, some of whom were present. This provoked supportive noises from Labour MPs and peers and dissenting noises from some of the Conservatives. However, music is banned during the speech, including '80s synth-pop, so you could hear cheers for peers and jeers for peers but not Tears for Fears.*

The speech is a list of bills the government will introduce, prefaced by the line 'my government will…' There are usually a couple of headline priorities and a catch-all promise of 'other measures' to offer flexibility to the government. Of course, the monarch does not write the speech. That is the job of the Prime Minister's political staff in No. 10, so you hear the incongruity of the monarch's deadpan delivery of political slogans better suited to an election hustings or TV debate:

> My government's priority is to deliver a national recovery from the pandemic that makes the United Kingdom stronger, healthier and more prosperous than before. To achieve this, my government will level up opportunities across all parts of the United Kingdom, supporting jobs, businesses and economic growth and addressing the impact of the pandemic on public services.

Or: 'My Lords and Members of the House of Commons, my government will govern in service to the country. My government's legislative programme will be mission-led and based upon the principles of security, fairness and opportunity for all.'

The Gracious Speech traditionally ends with the line, 'My

* This is a terrible joke, please remove it [ed.].

Lords and Members of the House of Commons, I pray that the blessing of Almighty God may rest upon your counsels.'

It's a grand affair, with lots of tradition, fripperies and hats.

THE LOYAL ADDRESS

In the House of Commons, once the Gracious Speech is over and MPs have assembled, a motion is moved and seconded by two government backbenchers. This 'Loyal Address' is something of an honour, and the two chosen ones are usually from different types of constituency and elected at different times.

Proposers and seconders on the Labour side have included Neil Kinnock, Robin Cook, Alun Michael and my first boss Ann Taylor; and for the Tories, Penny Mordaunt, Peter Lilley, Kenneth Baker and Kenneth Clarke. In May 2021, it was Shailesh Vara, MP for North West Cambridgeshire, and Katherine Fletcher, MP for South Ribble. In June 2001, it was Barry Sheerman and David Lammy. The first woman to speak on the Loyal Address was Conservative Florence Horsbrugh in November 1936. She was interviewed by BBC TV afterwards about the experience and thus became the first-ever MP to appear on television. The House of Commons Library has the list of proposers and seconders of the Loyal Address going back to May 1872 if you're really interested.

The tone for this speech is light-hearted, funny if possible, and not overburdened with ideological arguments.

It has to start with the motion itself:

I beg to move,

> That an humble address be presented to Her Majesty, as follows:
>
> Most Gracious Sovereign,
>
> We, Your Majesty's most dutiful and loyal subjects, the Commons of the United Kingdom of Great Britain and Northern Ireland, in Parliament assembled, beg leave to offer our humble thanks to Your Majesty for the Gracious Speech which Your Majesty has addressed to both Houses of Parliament.

Then ideally the MP talks about their constituency, some funny stories, a few in-jokes, and a little bit of self-effacing humour. Here's Frank Dobson MP in November 2009:

> I am honoured to be invited to open this debate and I am not the first from my constituency to do so. In 1906, this task fell to Sir Willoughby Hyett Dickinson. Conservative members will be pleased, but not surprised, to be told that he was an old Etonian. Liberal Democrat members will be pleased to know that he was a Liberal MP. Labour members will be even more pleased to learn that he later saw the light and joined the Labour Party.

You'll note the joke follows the time-honoured comedy rule of three, or 'trebling', with the pay-off on the third part (see later section on humour).

Here's Peter Dowd MP moving the loyal address in July 2024:

> It is worthwhile putting into context how I came to be moving the motion on the King's Speech this afternoon. Last Thursday morning, I was standing outside the Library minding my own business, watching somewhat bewildered hon. members wandering up and down the corridors, tentatively putting their heads into the odd room that may or may not have been a broom cupboard. And they were actually the returning members! I cannot imagine what it must have been like for the hundreds of new members. It brought back memories of when I undertook similar meanderings in the corridors of power.

And Florence Eshalomi MP, in seconding the motion, got this humorous remark in:

> This parliament sees a large churn of MPs, so may I take this opportunity to congratulate and welcome new members? Don't worry if you get lost; I have been here almost five years and I still get lost. My one piece of advice is this: make sure you know where Westminster Hall is, because you will always find the hon. Member for Strangford [Jim Shannon] there, on hand to point you in the right direction – after he has finished speaking in whatever debate is going on that day!

Eshalomi's speech was more serious-minded and political than Dowd's and provided an effective counterpoint. The choice of proposer and seconder is designed to give a platform to different MPs with a diversity of experiences.

Loyal Address checklist

- If you get the chance to give the Loyal Address, jump at it. It's a great honour
- It's a parliamentary event, so stick to the conventions and defer to tradition
- You should tell jokes, use anecdotes and pray-in-aid popular parliamentarians

SECOND READING DEBATES

As a bill passes through its stages in Parliament, the Second Reading is the first opportunity for MPs to make speeches about how they feel about whatever it says, or doesn't say. The debate is about the broad content of the bill, not specific amendments. It is the opportunity for the minister to set out the rationale for the change to the law and to explain the problem it aims to fix. It is also the opportunity for the opposition to state why the government is too timid, too short-sighted or just plain wrong. They then outline what they would do instead, which takes the form of a 'reasoned amendment'. A minister opens and closes the debate, and their opposition shadow speaks at the beginning and end.

Other members take part in the middle. This is the opportunity for backbench MPs to take part in a proper debate on a serious subject, in their role as lawmakers. They can highlight an issue of direct relevance to their constituency or a cause about which they care deeply. They can flag a concern about the proposed legislation, or spotlight a clause they especially favour. A Second Reading debate can be Parliament at its best.

When you are starting out, there's a tendency to overwrite a speech. Just because you have a firm grasp of an impressive range of rhetorical tools, you don't have to use them all, all of the time. If your speech sounds contrived, or over-complicated, or worse of all, like it's trying to be clever, you will lose your audience. Only the British have the expression 'too clever by half' because it is a deep-seated cultural trait that we despise a show-off.

In a Second Reading debate, for example, you might intend to nail one or two key ideas, showing your heartfelt opposition or warm support for the bill. Keep it simple. Choose the strongest points and the best arguments. Be prepared to leave material on the cutting room floor, even if you think it is fantastic. Kill your darlings, or at the very least put them in a cupboard for later.

It's all about striking the right tone. You are neither Martin Luther King at the Washington Monument nor Queen Elizabeth I at Tilbury. You are the honourable Member for Grantchester West. One of the subtle running gags in *Yes Minister* was when Jim Hacker grasped his lapels and slipped into Churchillian rhetoric when rehearsing his speeches. Don't try to be something you are not.

Don't get delusions of grandeur. Keep your feet firmly on the ground and your language in the realms of the mortal. To extend my tortured culinary metaphor, your dish needs simple themes, not every spice in the rack. Mixing in too much flavour just leaves a bad taste in the mouth.

There is a vote at the end, which the government must win for the bill to continue its passage.

Here's Alex Chalk, the Lord Chancellor and Justice Minister, opening the Second Reading of the Victims Bill in May 2024:

> I beg to move, that the bill be now read a second time.
>
> Some years ago, shortly before I entered Parliament, I was stood in the Crown court at Birmingham, having been instructed by the Crown Prosecution Service to prosecute five men accused of rape. It was alleged that they had groomed two young girls from Telford aged fifteen and sixteen and abducted them to Birmingham, where they subjected them to a weekend of degrading and humiliating sexual attacks, offering them up to their friends to do with as they pleased. What made the case even more chilling was that it was clear that the victims had been targeted because of their troubled backgrounds and sometimes challenging behaviour when interacting with authority figures such as the police. The defendants had made a cynical calculation that, if the girls ever did complain, they were unlikely to be believed. Well, they were believed. The jury got the measure of what had really gone on. After a fair trial, presided over by an independent judge, the defendants were all convicted of rape, robust sentences were passed and justice was done.
>
> I mention that at the beginning of this Second Reading debate because it provided me, and I hope now the House, with a powerful example of how supporting victims can make a decisive impact on outcomes. In that case, it was only because all the moving parts of the system came

> together to support those vulnerable girls to give their best evidence that a just outcome was delivered: conscientious police officers liaised sensitively with the young women to help them record their accounts; compassionate CPS lawyers and caseworkers applied for special measures to assist the victims to give evidence in court; and victim support staff worked hard during the tense days of the trial to assist victims with information and updates.
>
> Here is the central point: all those agencies recognised that, in order to deliver justice, victims must be treated not as mere spectators of the criminal justice system but as core participants in it. That is the mission of this government and of this bill. It will boost victims' entitlements; make victims' voices heard, including following a major incident like the tragedy of Grenfell or Hillsborough; and deliver further safeguards to protect the public.

This is as far as the minister got before the interventions started. It is customary for an MP speaking to 'give way' to interventions and to respond to them. If they are losing their way because of constant interventions, they may refuse to take many more interventions and say something like, 'I'd like to make some progress as time is tight.'

In July 2024, the Speaker reminded MPs: 'It is entirely at the discretion of the hon. member who has the floor to choose whether to give way. And once it is clear that the member does not wish to give way, colleagues should not persist in asking them to do so.'

Because interventions will come, the writers need to ensure their speeches have two things. The first is sections with breaks, where interventions can be taken, and the second is structure and signposting, so that the MP does not get thrown off track.

Once the frontbenchers have opened the debate, back-benchers can pile in. These speeches are usually a combination of speaking up for some aspect of the constituency and local institutions, supporting or opposing the bill and using external organisations' research to buttress the argument. The House of Commons Library provides a briefing for MPs ahead of a Second Reading debate, as do the political parties.

Then there are the many lobbyists' briefings targeted at MPs ahead of a Second Reading. For example, reading the Hansard of the Second Reading of the Levelling Up Bill in June 2022, you can see the influence of Greenpeace UK, the Home Builders Federation, the Institute of Economic Affairs (IEA), the Institute for Public Policy Research (IPPR), the Institute for Government (IfG) and the Nationwide Building Society, as well as the relevant reports from parliamentary select committees.

Writing a Second Reading speech, you should try to avoid the obvious citations and sources; try to use sources different to everyone else. You should use constituency-level data where possible and name-check local groups. You should make, if possible, a distinct argument about the bill, to stand out from the crowd. Mentioning specific parts of the bill, with clause numbers and page numbers, shows attention to detail and suggests you have actually read the bill in full. The closing speeches must address the points raised by other members. This is therefore a hard speech to write in advance, because much of it must be delivered in light of the actual debate. A skilful frontbencher will take a careful note of each contribution, clock the name of the MP's constituency and a key point from their speech. This is then played back in the wind-ups.

Here's Lord Parkinson in the House of Lords winding up on the Second Reading of the Media Bill:

> A number of noble Lords, including the noble Baronesses, Lady Kidron and Lady Foster, the right reverend Prelate the Bishop of Leeds, the noble Lord, Lord Hall of Birkenhead, focused on the changes to remit and the question of genres. I reassure noble Lords that the government recognise the importance of a diverse media sector in the UK, where audiences can select from a wide range of programmes, according to their own tastes and interests, and indeed to have those tastes and interests expanded. Our public service broadcasters have an important and distinctive role to play in helping to achieve that. To ensure that the regulatory framework supports these outcomes, the bill replaces the fourteen overlapping purposes and objectives to which public service broadcasters must contribute with a new, modernised remit. It is intended to provide a much clearer sense of our public service broadcasters' distinctive role in the sector.
>
> At the same time, it has always been our intention that the revised public service broadcasting framework,

> including the new remit, should retain the requirement on our public service broadcasters to produce a wide range of programmes. The government have listened to the views expressed by the Culture, Media and Sport Committee in another place; in particular, the committee's concerns that the remit is not clear enough on this point. As a result, as the noble Viscount, Lord Colville, noted, we have added an explicit requirement that our public service broadcasters should, together, continue to make a range of genres available.

You can see the minister adroitly naming each of his fellow peers who spoke and addressing the points they made. Once 'read a second time', the bill goes into its committee stage, where it is scrutinised line-by-line with the opportunity for amendments to the wording.

Second Reading speech checklist

- This is the chance to establish either support or opposition to a bill
- You must stick to the broad principles of the bill, not offer amendments
- Your speech must try to use new material and new angles on the subject, rather than regurgitating the lobbyists' briefings
- Unlike many parliamentary speeches, this one will have an audience of more than a couple of MPs. The House may be well populated for a Second Reading

WESTMINSTER HALL DEBATES

These are debates that are conducted in the Grand Committee Room, up some stairs off the magnificent medieval Westminster Hall (the bit that has survived both the fire and the Luftwaffe). It's a kind of overflow chamber that offers the space for more speeches to be made.

Unlike the gladiatorial face-off of the two sets of benches in the main Chamber, the MPs sit around a horseshoe-shaped table. This lends itself to more considered debating and a more collegiate vibe. MPs can apply to hold a thirty-, sixty- or ninety-minute debate through the Speaker's Office. There are no amendments and there are no votes. The MPs' deliberations end with the fact they have 'noted' the topic under discussion.

Westminster Hall debates take place on:

- Monday (if sitting): 4.30–7.30 p.m.
- Tuesday: 9.30–11.30 a.m. & 2.30–5.30 p.m.
- Wednesday: 9.30–11.30 a.m. & 2.30–5.30 p.m.
- Thursday: 1.30–4.30 p.m.

Finishing times in the afternoon may be later, depending on what's going on.

Westminster Hall debates create space for debating all kinds of issues. On 1 May 2024, Westminster Hall debated Chatham Docks, the Financial Conduct Authority, Youth Homelessness, Holiday Lettings and World ME Day.

Recent topics include:

- Dementia services
- Zero-emission buses
- Endometriosis education
- Knife crime awareness week
- Ehlers-Danlos syndrome and hypermobility spectrum disorders
- Support for bereaved children
- E-scooters: deaths and serious injuries

In writing the speech, you need to observe the protocols of moving the motion by saying, 'I beg to move, that this House has considered…' and introduce the topic. The first line is always, 'It is a pleasure to serve under your chairship.' You must then name the chair.

You can choose whether to say 'chairship' or 'chairmanship' or 'with you in the chair', depending on your preference.

For example, here's Debbie Abrahams MP starting off her Westminster Hall debate about dementia:

> I beg to move, that this House has considered inequalities in dementia services. It is a pleasure to serve under your chairship, Ms Rees. I thank the Backbench Business Committee for granting me this debate to discuss the huge inequalities in dementia diagnosis and other services across the country.

In July 2023, Abena Oppong-Asare MP raised the issue of

public access to defibrillators in Westminster Hall. Here's her speech, with the running commentary. One thing to note is the collaborative tone between MPs and the number of interventions during the speech.

> *Abena Oppong-Asare (Erith and Thamesmead) (Lab):* I beg to move, that this House has considered public access to defibrillators.
>
> It is a pleasure to serve under your chairship, Sir Charles [note the correct use of the protocol]. I am bringing this motion before the House this afternoon to maintain the steady pressure from campaigners and parliamentarians in relation to increasing awareness of and knowledge about defibrillators in two key regards: one, where they are; and two, how to use them [this is the *exordium*, or setting out of the argument]. This continues the fine work conducted by members from across this House, including the members of the all-party parliamentary group on defibrillators, its chair – the hon. Member for Stoke-on-Trent North [Jonathan Gullis] – and the hon. Member for Strangford [Jim Shannon], as well as members of the other place [it is a convention to thank other MPs who have worked on the issue].
>
> This issue was brought home to me by the experience of my constituent, Bonnie McGhee, who works in the cardiology unit at Queen Elizabeth Hospital. Sadly, Bonnie lost her father to a cardiac arrest but has since successfully raised funds for a defibrillator in his memory. Access to a defibrillator may have saved his life. The defibrillator that

Bonnie funded is in the Clockhouse Community Centre in memory of her father, Jeffrey Anthony Mee. I think of Bonnie and her late father often, and today, they are especially in my thoughts [this poignant anecdote makes the broader point].

In the UK, one person dies every three minutes from a heart or circulatory disease and, every year, 60,000 out-of-hospital cardiac arrests occur. Research by the National Institute for Health and Care Research found that only 8 per cent of people suffering a heart attack outside of hospital will survive. However, the same research found that the odds of survival increase to 32 per cent if a member of the public has access to an automated external defibrillator. If someone has access to a public defibrillator and can administer a life-saving electric shock to the heart to restore its normal rhythm, that will improve the likelihood of survival for anyone who has had a cardiac arrest.

Defibrillators represent an incredible technical advance. They are lightweight, easy to use and designed only to help and not harm the patient. The issue is not about their design but their distribution and public awareness of what they are and how to use them.

Virginia Crosbie (Ynys Môn) (Con):

I thank the hon. member for securing this important debate and for her excellent speech [this is the convention – to praise the speech]. Does she agree that community defibrillator training sessions are vital, and will she join me in thanking people such as Ryan Cawsey of St John Ambulance Cymru and Stephanie Roberts of the Gwalchmai Hotel, who make possible free defibrillator training sessions for Ynys Môn constituents?

Abena Oppong-Asare:
I thank the hon. member for her intervention, and I will come to that really important point about community training. I also thank her and agree with her comments about the charities and organisations that are already doing the groundwork to provide help and ensure that people are adequately trained. Research from Resuscitation Council UK shows that access to AEDs is not fairly distributed across the income and ethnic distribution of England. In other words, if someone is poor and/or black, they are less likely to have access to a defibrillator, but if someone is affluent and white, they are more likely to have access. The research shows unequal access across England, with fewer in the north-east and more in London. This is a classic example of what Dr Tudor Hart called 'inverse care law', whereby people with the most needs get the least provision, and vice versa. I hope that the minister can address that point and tell us what the government are doing to tackle these stark examples of health inequality.

Angus Brendan MacNeil (Na h-Eileanan an Iar) (SNP):
I am grateful to the hon. member for securing this important

debate. I want to mention Lucky2BHere, a charity based on the Isle of Skye that works across Na h-Eileanan an Iar and the Highlands. There are now more than 150 defibrillators across the Western Isles – my constituency – which is about the length of Wales. There is one outside my constituency office in Stornoway, which I will come back to in a second. They are outside schools, and can be accessed at all times.

The work is having to be done by volunteers, who see the great need for it. Michelle Macleod, who works in my office, collapsed in 2019 after having run a relay part of a half marathon, and it was with the help of defibrillators that her life was saved. That underscores, on a personal and an office basis, exactly how important those defibrillators are in my constituency. I congratulate the hon. member on raising this subject, so that there is greater awareness among the public and the government about what needs to be done.

Abena Oppong-Asare:
I thank the hon. member for making such an important contribution and Lucky2BHere for the work it is doing. I acknowledge his constituent, whose life was saved by this work. Volunteers are doing a lot of work to raise money for defibrillators. I have seen it happen in my constituency recently, where the Friends of Lesnes Abbey and Woods have raised money for defibrillators.

I welcome the minister's announcement that £1 million will be available for community defibrillators. I am sure that he will set out how that money will be used and what impact it will have. Otherwise, the money risks being more of a PR exercise than an exercise in serious public health policy.

Jim Shannon (Strangford) (DUP) [the inevitable intervention by Jim Shannon]:
I commend the hon. lady for securing the debate. She was very kind to mention me earlier – I brought the Automated External Defibrillators Bill to the House in 2020, as most members will know. The government accepted the need to have defibrillators in schools, which was really good.

The person who made that happen was Mark King, whose son Oliver died in March 2011 from a cardiac arrest – he was an outstanding young man who would have gone very far in the world. There have been 4,500 AEDs placed in schools, 70,000 staff have been trained in AED awareness and forty-seven lives have been saved. Two of the lives saved were in my constituency, because the defibrillators were in place at the right time. I congratulate the hon. lady on securing the debate, and I look forward to doing even more. Perhaps the minister can give an indication what the next steps will be.

Abena Oppong-Asare:
This is not to blow his trumpet, but I thank the hon. member for the work he has done on the issue and for the important points that he just highlighted.

Let me go back to my point about the minister's announcement of the £1 million that will be available for community defibrillators. I have questions about the timing of the announcement, just a few days ahead of this debate. What will the method of distribution be for the roll-out? I am concerned that ministers will pitch community groups against one another in a cruel competition to see who wins. The danger is that the winners are either the best organised or have the loudest voices, or else are favoured in the eyes of ministers. This does happen with schemes of this nature. Resuscitation Council UK warns about 'defibrillators being disproportionately stored in communities that have resources, amplifying the UK's mismatch between Automated External Defibrillator … density and Out of Hospital Cardiac Arrest incidence. By instead targeting public-access devices in areas of poor health and high OHCA incidence, this initiative could increase the chance of survival in the most high-risk communities.' There is also the issue of public awareness and knowledge. Each year, there are 60,000 out-of-hospital cardiac arrests in the UK, with less than one in ten surviving. While immediate CPR and defibrillation can more than double the chances of survival, public access defibrillators are used in less than one in ten cases. Defibrillators must be located in well-signposted, unlocked and easily accessible places that members of the community can access immediately in an emergency. They must be maintained and ready for use. By the way, the criminal justice system should throw the book at anyone convicted of vandalising public access defibrillators. Few crimes are more mindless than selfishly disabling a defibrillator that might save a stranger's life. Does the minister believe that the current range of punishments available to the courts for vandalising a defibrillator is adequate?

As the House will know, there is a national database of locations of defibrillators. It is called the Circuit and is maintained by the British Heart Foundation and the NHS. I pay tribute to Resuscitation Council UK and St John Ambulance for their work, but the database is not complete. The Circuit currently has more than 70,000 defibrillators mapped, but there are estimated to be between 100,000 and 200,000 devices in the UK. This means that emergency services, including the ambulance service, might not be able to direct people to a defibrillator to save someone's life. Will the minister explain how that can be acceptable and what the government are doing to rectify the situation?

Jim Shannon:

The hon. lady is right to outline the fact that many people do not necessarily know where defibrillators are located, and there is a need to ensure that that happens. Does she agree that one thing that should happen – maybe the minister can answer this question – is the teaching of CPR, which is crucial to ensuring that people feel confident enough to use the apparatus of a defibrillator? Does she feel that the minister should take that issue on board as well?

Abena Oppong-Asare:
I thank the hon. member for making such an important point. He literally took the words out of my mouth, because I was going to mention that later. He is right, because there is no point having all these defibrillators if no one knows how to use them. There are some located in my constituency and more widely, and people do not even know about them. I went to my local station recently, and some of the staff did not know that there was a defibrillator in the station. That lack of awareness is quite concerning.

I warmly welcome the Complete the Circuit campaign being run by the *Daily Express* and the British Heart Foundation. The campaign seeks to have every defibrillator listed. If Google Maps can list every pub and restaurant, which I know we all like, surely we should be able to see every defibrillator on our smartphones. I congratulate the *Daily Express* and its editor, Gary Jones, for this initiative – I think that is the first time I have ever said that.

I thank the *Daily Mirror*, which has run a lengthy campaign to install defibrillators in public spaces. Martin Bagot has been the driving force behind the campaign, and I know that people will be interested to know more about the current availability of defibrillators, such as the sorts of public venues that are more likely to have them and the public venues where there is an acute absence of them. Is the minister aware of any blackspots, particularly in rural areas, where there is a lack of defibrillators? As the hon. Member for Strangford mentioned, if someone can find a defibrillator, will they be able to use it?

There is a strong case for a public information campaign to explain what a defibrillator is and how to use it, which should be supported by workplace training courses and much greater awareness. There are examples of defibrillators from abroad where the information is much clearer and easier to understand. Can the minister tell us what assessment the department has made of accessibility for people who cannot read or who do not have English as their first language? Is there a case for reviewing signage and instructions to make defibrillators even more accessible?

Lastly, what about our workplace? According to information released under the Freedom of Information Act 2000, there are twenty-five defibrillators on the parliamentary estate, including in Central Lobby and Portcullis House – do we know where they are? No. We should be shouting that information from the rooftops; it should not be released through an FOI request. How many right hon. and hon. members know the whereabouts of those defibrillators? I do not know where the twenty-five are. How many of our staff know where they are? How many of us have had training in CPR or using defibrillators? This is a classic case of 'Physician, heal thyself'. In other words, we in this place should model good behaviour in all things, including access to defibrillators.

There are so many tragic stories from every constituency of lives lost when a defibrillator could have saved them, and I have heard some of them through interventions. Of course, there are many stories in which people have survived because of access to a defibrillator and the quick thinking and swift action of a stranger. That is the ultimate reminder that we are interconnected by shared humanity, that we rely on the kindness of strangers and that, one day, any one of us might need a passer-by to save our lives.

Sir Charles Walker (in the Chair):
I reassure the hon. member, as Chair of the Administration Committee as well as Chair of this proceeding, that we will certainly look at her request around defibrillators on the estate. An email is being sent to the Clerk now. I remind members who want to speak to bob up and down.

That last bit is significant. Within a day or two of the debate, signs went up across the Westminster estate highlighting the locations of the defibrillators, so the speech had an immediate impact.

Westminster Hall debates are a means to ventilate an issue, often very specific, in the presence of a minister. The minister's officials will be there in Westminster Hall. The minister's departmental civil servants will have written the speech, and that means civil servants have had to trawl through the corridors of power looking for things to say. An effective minister will have pushed the officials for something positive to say, perhaps using the speech as a hook for some kind of announcement. So while a Westminster Hall debate does not change the law, it can catalyse government action, secure a commitment to do something or at the very least shine some light on the issue under debate.

Westminster Hall speech checklist

- Westminster Hall is the overflow chamber where members can raise issues; it is the perfect arena to pursue campaigns and ensure some ministerial attention
- The speech should be passionate, informed and newsworthy
- You can invite constituents and campaigners to observe
- Get some friendly MPs on board to make the slot a bit more lively

ADJOURNMENT DEBATES

These are half-hour slots at the end of the parliamentary day when an MP can raise a specific issue and the minister must respond. Needless to say, ministers hate them because they involve time and effort and the danger of making an error. Departmental officials must draft around ten minutes of material (usually factual, flat and lifeless) and an effective minister peps it up a bit. A former minister told me the other day that he never used the officials' draft of a speech, but always wrote it into his own words. An official is usually placed in the Officials' Box for moral support, but a benevolent minister who feels that they are across their brief may let them have the night off.

The advantage for MPs is that they can ventilate a pressing issue for their constituents or a cause about which they are passionate, and get the points into Hansard. The debate cannot specifically call for changes to legislation and must be something for which a minister has responsibility (not congratulating your local football team or praising the winners of *Bake Off*).

Examples of adjournment debate topics include:

- Gypsies and Travellers (Andrew Selous MP)
- Dignity in Dying (Andrew Mitchell MP)
- Diversity in Public Appointments (Seema Malhotra MP)
- The Protection of Urban Trees (Catherine West MP)
- Ockenden Review of Maternity Care: Shrewsbury and Telford (Lucy Allan MP)

As an MP, you can apply to hold an adjournment debate to the Speaker's Office on a Wednesday for the following Tuesday to Monday. The Speaker gets to choose the Thursday debate, and for other days, the adjournment debate is decided by a ballot.

Like Groundhog Day, the motion, moved by a whip instead of the sponsoring MP, is the same every time: 'That this House do now adjourn.' But the topics then debated can be weird and wonderful. The speeches follow the same format. The MP speaks, the minister responds, the Chamber is almost empty, and the whole thing is over in thirty minutes. Other MPs may make speeches or interventions to make their points, support their friend or to shoehorn themselves into Hansard with minimal effort.

The Chamber is sparsely populated for adjournment debates. There may be only the MP making their speech, the minister and one or two others. There's no vote, and nothing will happen as a result of the debate, so MPs are elsewhere going about their business. Unfortunately, to the untrained eye it therefore looks like MPs 'don't care' about the issue, which results in keyboard warriors posting nonsense about MPs ignoring the NHS or whatever the topic may be.

If you're a backbencher who wants to make a speech in another MP's adjournment debate, you need to ask permission from the MP whose debate it is and the minister responding. The government Whips' Office will tell you which lucky junior minister has drawn the short straw. If they agree to you taking up a slice of their fifteen minutes of fame, you must let the Speaker's Office know with an email or note. Far more effective, however, is to just intervene in the speeches, which requires no permission, and very few MPs will be present to compete for time. In order to do this, though, you must be present from the start of the debate, or you won't be able to speak, as this exchange during Henry Smith MP's adjournment debate on duty-free shopping in September 2023 shows:

> *Sir William Cash (Stone):*
> Will my hon. friend give way?
>
> *Madam Deputy Speaker (Dame Rosie Winterton):*
> Order. No. The hon. gentleman has only just come into the Chamber. This is an adjournment debate, and he should have been here from the beginning to intervene, as he knows.
>
> *Henry Smith:*
> I did not notice my hon. friend slink in behind me, but I am grateful for his moral support, Madam Deputy Speaker, even though by your order he is unable to vocalise it.

That's him told.

The undisputed King of the Intervention is the DUP MP Jim Shannon, who has made hundreds of interventions on every topic under the sun. The man has a view on everything, from school funding in North Northumberland to Cornwall's dark skies. Here he is intervening on Lucy Allen MP's debate about her local maternity services:

Lucy Allen (Telford) (Con):

The interim findings in the Ockenden review were not published, and I understand that the hospital trust has not been told about them. The families were certainly not told about them, and neither were MPs. There has been no statement to the House, and we do not know what action is being taken to ensure the safety of women and babies at Shrewsbury and Telford Hospital NHS Trust.

Jim Shannon (Strangford) (DUP):

I am an avid watcher of that Sunday night programme *Call the Midwife* – I am not sure whether you watch it, Mr Speaker – where everything seems to work out at the end of the day. The hon. lady is outlining something that does not work out at the end of the day. She mentioned families. Does she agree that the care of mother and baby must be a priority, and that more support for mothers who have had several children must be considered, to ensure that they are coping and not expected simply to carry on because they already know what to expect? Every life is precious and adds more pressures to families, particularly mothers.

Lucy Allan:
I very much appreciate the hon. gentleman's intervention. As always, he makes an excellent point, and I am grateful to him for his many interventions in many debates I have secured.

She said through gritted teeth.

Here's an example of an effective adjournment debate from 17 May 2024, when the MP for Cities of London and Westminster Nickie Aitken raised the issue of British Muslims being conned and ripped off when they make the Hajj (the pilgrimage to Mecca). It's a typical adjournment debate. A specialist topic. A speech by the MP, a reply from the minister and one intervention from a friendly MP. Not much soaring oration, but a meat-and-drink example of Parliament at work. Here it is (with my running commentary):

Nickie Aiken (Cities of London and Westminster) (Con):
I am proud to represent nearly 15,000 Muslims as their MP in Parliament. The all-party parliamentary group on British Muslims recently informed me that my constituency has the seventieth-largest Muslim population in the country [probably a research paper issued to all MPs with constituency figures. Always the best way to get your research into the mouth of an MP], and I know from my time as a

Westminster City councillor, and now as an MP, of the key role that British Muslims play in making the two cities such a proudly multicultural and welcoming place in which to live.

Since being elected, I have worked with a large number and a wide variety of organisations in my constituency, including those supporting my Muslim constituents, such as the Westminster Bangladeshi Welfare Trust and the Westminster Bangladeshi Association, both of which have supported their communities for many years. Last month I was delighted to be invited to attend Eid celebrations on the Churchill Gardens Estate in Pimlico, organised by the residents' association, led by their impressive chairman Christina Walsh [it's always a good idea to name specific constituency people, places and organisations]. The event brought together local people of all faiths and none to celebrate this deeply significant religious festival, enabling us to enjoy it as a community no matter what our background. It was a very special afternoon, and I was delighted to be able to continue to learn more about the Ummah community and, in turn, about the Hajj journey that so many of my constituents will make next month [this peroration is all about establishing the speaker's credentials to speak on this topic and prove their *ethos*].

Let me explain to those who do not already know that Hajj is the pilgrimage to the holy city of Mecca in Saudi Arabia, the birthplace of the prophet Mohammed, which every adult Muslim is expected to undertake in his or her lifetime if financially and physically able to do so. From speaking to Muslim friends about their experiences of Hajj, I know what a special and significant time it is for them. Hajj is the fifth of the fundamental Muslim practices known as the five pillars of Islam, and is obligatory. The pilgrim rites begin on the seventh day of Dhu Al-Hijjah, the last month of the Islamic year, and end on the twelfth day. As it is based on the lunar calendar, this year Hajj is expected to begin on 14 June and conclude on 19 June.

Despite its religious importance, many travelling from the UK to Mecca to perform Hajj are sadly not immune to targeting by fraudsters. I learned at first hand about Hajj-related fraud on a recent visit to the City of London Police, based in my constituency, where I met Commander Umer Khan [more name checks]. The City of London Police take the national lead on fraud, and thus Hajj-related fraud court cases come under its jurisdiction. Commander Khan is leading the force's nationwide efforts to highlight how to prevent being a victim of Hajj-related fraud, and I would like to take this opportunity to thank him and his team for their outstanding work.

According to the police, only 3 per cent of Hajj-related fraud is actually reported [this is a good example of a 'killer fact': something that stands out and makes the point, rather than a slew of figures that are hard to get hold of]. The reasons for such low reporting can be multifaceted. Some may not wish to report the crime as they booked through a contact of someone they know in their community or from their mosque; others may wish not to complain due to embarrassment or shame. We often hear these reasons from victims of whatever fraud, in whatever circumstances. One of the reasons I applied for this debate is to send a clear message to our British Muslim community that they should feel safe and confident that they will be taken seriously if they report a suspected fraud. Due to the low levels of reporting, we simply cannot know the full extent of what I think is a heinous crime.

In my discussions with City of London Police officers about Hajj-related fraud, they informed me that they have accidentally come across incidences of fraud, but are finding it increasingly difficult to receive reports of this crime.

Mr Jonathan Lord (Woking) (Con):
My hon. friend is making an eloquent speech. As a former deputy leader of Westminster City Council, I know the importance of the Muslim community there, just as I have an important Muslim community in Woking. My hon. friend is making a good point: the message must go out to Members of this House that we should speak with religious and community leaders locally to ensure that this heinous crime is reported. As I say, I have a large Muslim community, but I have not heard of this before. It sounds terrible. [This is a largely pointless intervention that adds little. But it gives Lord something to show to his constituents. Woking is the home to the first-ever purpose-built mosque in the UK, which I would have mentioned if I'd written this intervention.]

Nickie Aiken:

My hon. friend is absolutely right. Before I went on my visit with the City of London Police, which takes the lead on this, and met Commander Khan, I was not aware of it either. It is important that we highlight these hidden crimes. I would like to take this opportunity to congratulate my hon. friend on securing his third Private Members' Bill of his political career so far [she's referring to Lord's success with his Private Members' Bill to require operator licences authorising the carrying out of spaceflight activities to specify the licensee's indemnity limit. In Woking, they speak of little else].

I want to highlight the importance of ensuring that members of the Muslim community in this country know that if they are victims of any type of fraud, but particularly Hajj-related fraud, they can inform the police and have it investigated properly. The City of London Police believe that one of the reasons for low levels of reporting may be traditional attitudes that persist: having become 'pure' as a Hajji, the person involved may not want to speak of such worldly things as fraud on their pilgrimage. Those who suspect that they have been a victim of any type of fraud should report it straightaway to Action Fraud, the national fraud and cyber-crime reporting service, which is available online at actionfraud.police.uk.

Every year, 25,000 British Muslims travel to Mecca in Saudi Arabia to undertake their Hajj. Many will have saved for years in the knowledge that it will be a once-in-a-lifetime trip. Brits who take part in the pilgrimage spend a combined £125 million each year. These costs include return flights, accommodation, and paying for a guide. Data obtained from the police.uk website shows that, sadly, police forces have reported Hajj-related fraud where British citizens have lost anything from £1,000 up to a staggering £33,000 to fraudsters, who promised to arrange their Hajj travel and accommodation but had no intention of ever doing so and were never heard from again.

Those shopping around for the best deal for their trip to Mecca, both in their local community and increasingly online – particularly on social media – have been attracted to packages covering flights, accommodation and visas, which appear to offer good value for money. Some rogue operators advertise large reductions on what would usually be charged. Accommodation advertised as a four-star hotel is, in reality, on arrival found to be barely the quality of a one-star place. I have heard reports of flights being deliberately over-subscribed, leading to people failing to make the trip at all, and of people posing as travel agents, charging extortionate prices for visas – up to £1,000 each – when they are actually free. I have heard of travellers being asked to pay in cash or make a direct bank transfer prior to their trip and being told that they would receive their tickets and travel documents nearer to the departure date, never to be received. A once-in-a-lifetime trip, often using life savings, ends in heartbreak. I cannot imagine the distress and upset that must cause people so looking forward to undertaking their Hajj [these are all good anecdotal examples that support the main argument. Case studies bring the speech to life, and might make good stories for the local media].

As we lead up to this year's Hajj, I thought it important to highlight the dangers that fraudsters can pose to our citizens at this special time, and to ensure that people know that there is a way to protect themselves from becoming victims of Hajj-related fraud. In response to tackling this fraud, which affects not just British Muslims but those planning their pilgrimage from across the world, the Saudi Arabian government have acted decisively. It is important to highlight that this is a global fraud issue. I read with interest in *Arab News* yesterday that the Iraqi authorities have prosecuted more than twenty-five companies fraudulently engaging in commercial Hajj operations.

In 2022, knowing that Hajj-related fraud was increasingly an issue, the Saudi Arabian Ministry of Hajj and Umrah created the Nusuk Hajj portal, which has changed the way that individuals book their pilgrimage. The portal is available in over fifty countries, including the United Kingdom, and was created to provide a seamless and safe pilgrimage booking experience. By centralising the process by which visas are acquired, much of the fraud has been stifled, thankfully. It is imperative that individuals book their Hajj trips only through the Nusuk portal. Anyone posing as a provider of visas or trips to Mecca for Hajj is simply misleading people.

Sadly, even after the creation of the Nusuk Hajj portal and despite its success in reducing fraud, the criminal fraternity continues – as it always does – to attempt to find new avenues to try to take advantage. My advice to Hajjis is to remain vigilant about what is being sold and by whom. I still receive reports of individuals being sold Umrah visas and generic tourist visas and being told that they are acceptable for their Hajj pilgrimage. That is not the case. People can only travel with a Hajj visa from the Nusuk portal. The other visas allow access at any other time of year, but for Hajj period, those reliant on those visas will not be permitted entry to Mecca.

It is important to note that Hajj-related fraud is not just about people buying a package that simply does not exist; it also involves profiteering from a sacred pilgrimage. The fraudsters involved are, to my mind, the lowest of the low. I thank the groups that work tirelessly to highlight the importance of protecting people from Hajj-related fraud and encouraging the use of the Nusuk Hajj portal. As well as Commander Khan and the City of London Police, I must thank the hon. Member for Bolton South East (Yasmin Qureshi) for her work leading the all-party parliamentary group on Hajj and Umrah, which, alongside the Council for British Hajjis, has raised the profile of this fraud immeasurably.

I met the hon. member recently to discuss Hajj-related fraud, and she was clear that trading standards departments up and down the country, and specifically in Birmingham, have worked hard to uncover such criminal activity, bring those involved to justice, and ensure that the wider Muslim community is aware of possible fraud and the importance of using the Nusuk Hajj portal. By highlighting and encouraging the use of the portal among British Muslims, I hope that we can tackle Hajj-related fraud once and for all. After all, this is UK Finance's Take Five Week – a week designed to raise awareness of and help tackle all types of fraud. [This is a well-constructed speech with the right amount of detail and information. The MP and her team have put some effort into the research.]

I look forward to hearing from the minister how his department and the government in general will support British Muslims this year and every year to ensure that they can enjoy their pilgrimage without fear of exploitation and disappointment.

The Minister for Crime, Policing and Fire (Chris Philp): Let me start by thanking my hon. friend the Member for Cities of London and Westminster [Nickie Aiken] and congratulating her on securing this afternoon's adjournment debate. I think she first raised the topic in business questions on 18 April, and here we are just a few weeks later debating it [the minister thinks this because his officials have told him]. She is right to raise the issue, particularly given that it is just a few weeks until Muslims from all over the world will travel to Saudi Arabia for Hajj. That will of course include thousands of British Muslims. For many, their pilgrimage is a once-in-a-lifetime opportunity.

My hon. friend set out clearly the way that Hajj fraud

operates [this is code for 'the MP has said pretty much everything I was going to read out from my briefing note, but I'm going to repeat it anyway']. Exploitative criminals prey on hard-working families to dupe them out of their money, sometimes using fake websites and other means to persuade people to pay for goods or services that are not forthcoming. I echo [repeat] the advice that my hon. friend gave people to make sure that they book visas only via the properly authorised route. When booking travel via a travel agent, it is essential to make sure that the travel agency or tour operator is a member of the Association of British Travel Agents, to carefully check online reviews, to make sure that the travel company is ATOL-protected by the Civil Aviation Authority, and to make sure that the flight details and Hajj visa are valid. Those are all steps that people can and should take to protect themselves and make sure the counterparty they are dealing with is a legitimate organisation. We also strongly advise people never to pay by cash or by direct bank transfer into someone's personal bank account.

The government are committed to tackling both Hajj fraud and fraud more widely. I am pleased to report that overall, fraud is falling, with the latest data from the crime survey for England and Wales showing a 16 per cent reduction year on year. But I am afraid to say that fraud remains the most common crime type, accounting for about 37 per cent of all crime. That means that one in every eighteen adults was a victim of fraud in the last year. That is why we must clamp down on all forms of fraud, including Hajj fraud.

That is encapsulated in our fraud strategy, published almost exactly a year ago, which entails investing about £100 million to improve law enforcement capabilities and launching a new national fraud squad, with 400 specialist investigators in post. It also includes steps to replace the Action Fraud service this year, which has been the subject of some criticism, to ensure victims of fraud have the confidence to come forward knowing their case will be dealt with properly.

We are also cracking down on fraudsters online. We know that many cases of Hajj fraud have an online element, which requires particular vigilance. When the Online Safety Act 2023 is fully enacted, it will help the regulator Ofcom to hold to account online social media platforms if they allow fraud to proliferate. That will take time to come into force fully, so to protect people even sooner, we have agreed the online fraud charter with twelve of the largest tech companies, including Amazon, eBay, Meta and Google. That was entered into last November and includes a series of voluntary actions that they will take. When the 2023 Act comes fully into force, it will compel large social media platforms to take proactive steps to combat fraud, including Hajj fraud.

As my hon. friend said, public awareness is critical, as is people taking steps to protect themselves. That is why the 'Stop! Think Fraud' national behaviour change campaign is so important. It encourages the public to always stop and think before they make a payment, and ask themselves, 'Is it possible I am being defrauded? Is the counterparty legitimate? What can I do to check their credentials before making that payment?' Criminals are becoming increasingly sophisticated, often now using artificial intelligence to generate images or even videos designed to trick people into paying money. The public's vigilance is therefore extremely important, alongside the law enforcement response through the fraud strategy and the actions we are taking to compel large online platforms to be more proactive in stopping fraud proliferating online. [These are the standard lines to take from the Department, inserted into the speech.]

In conclusion, I am very grateful to my hon. friend for raising this issue on behalf of her Muslim communities in the Cities of London and Westminster. My hon. friend the Member for Woking (Mr Lord) raised the issue on behalf of the Muslim communities in his constituency [it is a parliamentary convention to name members who have made a contribution and say something positive]. In my own constituency of Croydon South, there is a significant Muslim community too. I know that other members with Muslim communities will echo the call made by my two hon. friends for our constituents to be vigilant and to report immediately any suspicious activity. Hajj fraud is a disgraceful example of criminals exploiting a religious pilgrimage for their own personal gain. I am sure all of us condemn that wholeheartedly and will do everything we possibly can to stop it.

This is an effective speech because it contains a central argument that runs through the spine of the speech. The speaker is clear on what they are saying and the underpinning rationale. She establishes her credentials to speak (her '*ethos*') on the topic early on in her *exordium* and uses local organisations and figures to pray-in-aid for her argument. The speech uses anecdotes and statistics to support the argument. This MP is clear in her argument and her demands from the minister.

This adjournment debate took place on a Friday because of the impending general election. It started at 2.32 p.m. and ended at 2.52 p.m. Twenty minutes of speeches, but a lot more time to research, draft and promote the speech and the topic it covers.

Adjournment debate checklist

- Choose a topic that is timely, relevant and something you care about
- Write a ten-minute speech
- Use plenty of local examples, anecdotes and case studies
- Name-check some local figures and organisations
- Encourage some friendly MPs to spare thirty minutes to show support
- Wait for the inevitable intervention by Jim Shannon

PRIVATE MEMBERS' BILLS

A Private Members' Bill is a bill introduced by a backbench MP to change some aspect of the law or introduce a new one. The members who get to introduce a Private Members' Bill are selected by a ballot. The bill only stands a chance if the government makes the time available to pass it. Yet this is sometimes the route to change the law.

In the 2022–23 session of Parliament, sixteen bills from the Private Members' Bill ballot became law:

1. Carer's Leave Act 2023
2. Child Support (Enforcement) Act 2023
3. Child Support Collection (Domestic Abuse) Act 2023
4. Co-operatives, Mutuals and Friendly Societies Act 2023
5. Electricity Transmission (Compensation) Act 2023
6. Employment (Allocation of Tips) Act 2023
7. Employment Relations (Flexible Working) Act 2023
8. Equipment Theft (Prevention) Act 2023
9. Neonatal Care (Leave and Pay) Act 2023
10. Offenders (Day of Release from Detention) Act 2023
11. Powers of Attorney Act 2023
12. Protection from Redundancy (Pregnancy and Family Leave) Act 2023
13. Protection from Sex-based Harassment in Public Act 2023
14. Shark Fins Act 2023
15. Supported Housing (Regulatory Oversight) Act 2023
16. Worker Protection (Amendment of Equality Act 2010) Act 2023

Another method of introducing a Private Members' Bill is under the Ten Minute Rule. Ten Minute Rule Bills are a kind of Private Members' Bill introduced in the House of

Commons under Standing Order No. 23. The Ten Minute Rule means a backbench MP can make his or her case for a new bill. The speechwriter must draft a speech lasting, naturally, no more than ten minutes. An opposing speech may also be made before the House decides whether the bill should be introduced.

The speech for a Private Members' Bill is snappy and short, and it picks up the reasons to support or oppose it, or merely raise concerns.

In February 2024, Laurence Robertson MP proposed his bill to give financial support to people who are terminally ill. This is the opening section:

> I beg to move, that the bill be now read a second time.
>
> This very small bill is narrow in scope, but it will provide financial assistance and fairness to people who are terminally ill who have seen the sponsors of their pension schemes become insolvent. It will do that by changing the definition of 'terminally ill' for this purpose. I thank the legislative team of the Department for Work and Pensions and my staff for their help preparing the bill.
>
> I think everyone in the House would agree that those who receive the devastating news that they have a terminal illness should receive as much financial help as possible in their final days. The loss of their right to pension payments is a blow that they should not have to suffer, and that is what the bill seeks to address.
>
> By way of background, the bill focuses on the Pension

Protection Fund and the Financial Assistance Scheme. The Pension Protection Fund was established by the Pensions Act 2004 and pays compensation to individuals when the sponsors of defined benefit pension schemes – usually their employers – become insolvent and lack the necessary assets to pay those pensions to the level that the Pension Protection Fund would ordinarily pay. That applies to insolvency that has taken place on or after 6 April 2005. The Financial Assistance Scheme applies to individuals whose pension schemes were unable to meet their pension liabilities in full if those schemes started to wind up between 1 January 1997 and 5 April 2005.

The bill relates to compensation payments from those schemes made to people with terminal illness. When meeting the liabilities of pension schemes, the Pension Protection Fund can pay a one-off lump sum to someone who is terminally ill. The Financial Assistance Scheme can start to make pension payments, but not pay a lump sum, to someone at any age with a terminal illness. The issue is the definition of a terminal illness.

This speech establishes the scope of the bill, the reasons why it is needed and how it would work. It is a good example of very targeted and specific legislative change. It reminds me of William Blake's view that 'he who would do good to another must do it in Minute Particulars: general Good is the plea of the scoundrel, hypocrite, and flatterer'. A good MP can make small changes to the benefit of the many.

Private Members' Bill speech checklist

- These are a fantastic opportunity for MPs to right wrongs, shine a light on injustice and change the world by inches
- Choose the content well, presenting a combination of new data, stories, rhetorical flourishes and a strong argument for your bill
- Negotiate with the government whips and see if you can get ministers' support to make your great idea into an actual law

SPEAKING IN A NO-CONFIDENCE DEBATE

Our constitution stipulates that the governing party or parties must enjoy the confidence of the majority of the House of Commons. That means 50 per cent-plus-one of the MPs in the Commons, minus Sinn Féin (who don't attend) and the Speaker and his or her deputies. A parliamentary wheeze is to try to bring down a government with a 'no-confidence' motion to test the strength of support for the governing party(s). This might be brought by the opposition, or the government (to prove a point). Since 1895, no-confidence debates have brought down a government only four times: in 1895, twice in 1924, and in 1979, when Callaghan lost the vote by one.

In January 2019, the Conservative MP and minister Michael Gove spoke for the government in the winding-up speeches in a Labour-inspired motion of no-confidence in Prime Minister Theresa May. He used a combination of excoriating wit and invective to reframe the motion from no confidence in May to no confidence in the then-Leader of the Opposition, Jeremy

Corbyn. At times, members of the Labour front bench struggled not to laugh.

Building up a case that Corbyn was unfit to lead the country on grounds of national security, he prefigured many of the arguments used in Labour's defeat in the general election in December that year. So complete was Gove's reframing, he hardly mentions the actual target of the motion – Theresa May – at all. It is all about Corbyn's record on national security.

The term 'barnstorming' was widely deployed to describe Gove's speech. The idiom is taken from travelling theatre troupes in the USA, entertaining rural audiences in their barns with bawdy plays. Barnstorming was then used to describe political campaigns and later aerobatic displays by daredevil pilots. There's a touch of all three in Gove's speech – but how does he do it?

> Perhaps the bravest and the finest speech that came from the opposition benches was given by the Member for Barrow-in-Furness. It takes courage – and he has it, having been elected on a Labour mandate representing working-class people – to say that the leader of the party that he joined as a boy is not fit to be Prime Minister. He speaks for his constituents, and he speaks for the country.
>
> That takes me to the speech from the shadow Secretary of State, the hon. Member for West Bromwich East [Tom Watson]. He spoke well, but I felt he did not rise to the level of events [to damn an opponent with faint praise, as the philosopher Favorinus stated, is more powerful than an

outright assault]. One thing that was characteristic about his speech is that he did not once mention the Leader of the Opposition or why he should be Prime Minister [this is rich given that Gove does not mention May or why she should continue as Prime Minister. I think the psychiatrists call this 'projection'].

I have a lot of time for the honourable member, and we have several things in common: we both lost weight recently – him much more so; we are both friends of Israel – him much more so; and we both recognise that the Member for Islington North is about the worst possible person to lead the Labour Party [this device is called *anapodoton*. The idea is that the speaker leaves something unsaid, which the audience fills in in their own minds. Gove builds anticipation with the phrase 'him much more so' used twice, and because we expect things in threes, we fill in the gap. The phrase has impact because Gove is highlighting divisions between the leader and deputy leader of the Labour Party].

As well as great speeches from the back benches, we also have some interesting speeches from the front benches. We had a speech of over twenty minutes from my great friend [this is irony; they are not great friends] the leader of the Scottish National Party in this place, the right hon. Member for Ross, Skye and Lochaber [Ian Blackford]. Again, however, in those twenty minutes he did not once mention the Common Fisheries Policy. I think everyone in Scotland who recognises the potential to free ourselves from the

Common Fisheries Policy that Brexit provides will note that in twenty minutes of precious parliamentary time, the SNP did not mention them, is not interested in them and, as far as the fishing people of Scotland are concerned, literally has nothing to say.

I must now turn to the speech from the leader of the Liberal Democrats, the right hon. Member for Twickenham [Sir Vince Cable], someone for whom I also have affection and respect [no he doesn't; more irony]. He made a number of good points, but he also said that he regretted the referendum. This from the party that was the first in this House to say that we should have a referendum on EU membership. Because he doesn't like the result of the last referendum, he now wants another referendum. The Liberal Democrat policy on referendums is not the policy of Gladstone or Lloyd George. It's the policy of Vicky Pollard: 'No but, yeah but, no but, yeah.' [This is called an allusion – a reference to a work of literature, theatre, poetry or music, or in this case, television comedy.]

I should also commend the speech given by the leader of the Democratic Unionist Party in this place, the right hon. Member for Belfast North [Nigel Dodds]. He explained that he had been inundated with text messages today from people in this House saying, 'Please, please, please back the government tonight.' And some of those text messages had even come from Conservatives.

Critically, when we think about confidence in this country and in this government, I think a daily vote of confidence is being executed by the individuals investing in this country, creating jobs and opportunity for all our citizens. Under this government, this country remains the most successful country for foreign direct investment of any country in Europe, with more than £1,300 billion being invested in the last year. That is why *Forbes* magazine says that this country is the best destination for new jobs in the world [this is an argument using an appeal to authority *argumentum ab auctoritate* – in this case, *Forbes* magazine. MPs use external sources of evidence all the time, but in philosophical terms to appeal to authority is a logical fallacy].

It is why the independent organisation JLL says that the best place in the world for the future of services is here in the United Kingdom. It is why, once again, London has been recorded by independent inspectors as the best place in the world for tech investment. We see that when the Spanish rail firm Talgo shortlists six destinations for investment in new rolling stock, and all six are in the United Kingdom; when Boeing opens a new factory in Sheffield to create jobs for British workers; when Chanel moves from France to London to establish a new corporate headquarters, and when Starbucks moves from Amsterdam to London in order to ensure more investment in jobs. The Opposition should wake up and smell the coffee. [The bar for parliamentary humour is set low. This just about passes the test.]

All this – in the words of the BBC – 'despite Brexit'. That investment – those jobs that have been created under my right honourable friend the Prime Minister's inspirational leadership – has been made in public services and social justice. As we heard, from my hon. friends the Members for Dudley South [Mike Wood] and for Bexhill and Battle [Huw Merriman], there are 1.9 million more children in good or outstanding schools. It is also the case that the gap between the poorest and the richest in our schools has narrowed under this Conservative government. We have a record level of investment in the NHS and, thanks to my right hon. friend the Secretary of State for Health and Social Care, a ten-year plan and £20 billion of investment – £394 million extra every week – for our NHS.

We also have investment in our national security. We meet the 2 per cent target for investment in NATO and we have two new aircraft carriers, which are capable of projecting British force and influence across the world in defence of freedom and democracy. By contrast, while we are standing up for national security, what about the right hon. Member for Islington North? He wants to leave NATO. He wants to get rid of our nuclear deterrent [this is called *hypophora* – asking a question and then immediately answering it. This is distinct from the famous rhetorical question that is asked but not answered by the speaker, designed to make the listener answer it in their own mind].

He said recently in a speech, 'Why do countries boast about the size of their armies? That is quite wrong. Why don't we emulate Costa Rica, which has no army at all?' No allies, no deterrent, no army [a good old-fashioned tricolon, or group of three] – no way can this country ever allow that man to be our Prime Minister and in charge of our national security.

If the Leader of the Opposition cannot support our fighting men and women, who does he support? Who does he stand beside? It was fascinating to discover that he was there when a wreath was laid to commemorate those who were involved in the massacre of Israeli athletes at the Munich Olympics. He says he was present but not involved. 'Present but not involved' sums him up when it comes to national security.

When this House voted to bomb the fascists of ISIS after an inspirational speech by the right hon. Member for Leeds Central [Hilary Benn], sixty-six Labour members, including the hon. Member for West Bromwich East, voted with this government to defeat fascism. I am afraid the Leader of the Opposition was not with us. In fighting fascism, he was present but not involved.

Similarly, when this House voted to take the action necessary when Vladimir Putin executed an act of terrorism on our soil, many good Labour members stood up to support what we were doing, but not the Leader of the Opposition.

[At this point, there was an interjection from Danielle Rowley on a point of order, namely that Gove's speech was irrelevant and dangerous. It was rejected.]

If the Leader of the Opposition will not stand up against Putin when he attacks people in this country, if he will not stand up against fascists when they are running riot in Syria, if he will not stand up for this country when the critical national security questions are being asked, how can we possibly expect him to stand up for us in European negotiations?

Will he stand up for us against Spain over Gibraltar? Will he stand up against the commission to ensure that we get a good deal? Of course he will not, because he will not even stand up for his own Members of Parliament.

Why is it that a Labour Member of Parliament needs armed protection at her own party conference? Why is it that nearly half of female Labour MPs wrote to the Leader of the Opposition to say that he was not standing up against the vilification and the abuse that they received online, which had been carried out in his name? If he cannot protect his own Members of Parliament, if he cannot protect the proud traditions of the Labour Party, how can he possibly protect this country? [This is a rhetorical question which presupposes a negative response – a device called *erotesis*.]

We cannot have confidence in him to lead. We have confidence in this government, which is why I commend this motion to the House.

This motion of no-confidence in the Conservatives rebounded spectacularly on the Labour leadership. Gove uses a range of rhetorical devices to make an entertaining and well-turned speech, but far more effective is the central device of turning the tables on his opponents. Instead of a speech defending his boss, Gove reframes the debate into a motion of no-confidence in the Leader of the Opposition. With unerring political instinct, Gove understood that the majority of Labour MPs had little or no confidence in Jeremy Corbyn, and so highlighted his enemy's weaknesses. This is known as punching the bruise.

This one, on the other hand, brought by the Conservative opposition in March 1979 against the Labour government led by James Callaghan, landed. Here's Margaret Thatcher's peroration on that fateful occasion:

> Go anywhere in the country, and one finds that the demand is for two things – less tax and more law and order. The phrase 'law and order' does not refer only to vandalism and violence [alliteration] – although that is uppermost in many people's minds. It means that our citizens expect and are not getting an ordered or orderly society. They expect the rubbish to be cleared, the schools to be open and the hospitals to be functioning. They are not. They expect each man and woman to rise to his obligations in an orderly and decent way. They expect bargains to be kept between trade unions and employers. Finally, they expect ministers to support them in those views.
>
> In the recent closure of schools, the authorities did not support the law-abiding citizen or his children. It was the citizens who had to go to the courts when their children were denied access to the schools. It was the law that upheld the parents when they could not persuade the council or ministers to help them. The Secretary of State for Education took the view – astonishing as it may seem – that the council had not failed to discharge its duty. The right hon. lady has been prepared to pass new laws to close good schools.

It is a pity that she has not been as eager to use existing laws to keep present schools open.

At least there was a law to invoke. There are many cases when the interests or livelihood of a person can be changed or taken away and there is no remedy at law. That is the legacy of this government. After five years, it is not surprising that our people want the benefit of a government who regard the maintenance of the rule of law as the foremost of their tasks.

There we have the record, and some of the reasons for failure. Each crisis, industrial or financial has been met by short-term measures, but there has been no serious attempt to deal with the underlying problems. On the contrary, they are worse.

The government have doubled prices, doubled dole queues, doubled debt, diminished our defences and undermined public respect and confidence in the law [this is *anaphora*, or repetition at the start of the sentence, and alliteration on the d words]. There has been a failure not only of policies but of the whole philosophy on which they are based – the philosophy which elevates the state, dwarfs the individual and enlarges the bureaucracy. Across the western world, the tide is turning against that, and soon the same thing will happen here [how very prescient].

I return to the occasion for this motion, which arose out of a constitutional matter affecting the whole House. [Thatcher started her speech with reference to the devolution referendums in Scotland and Wales and now returns to them. This is called a 'call-back'.] Hon. members from both sides made an eminently reasonable request to the Prime

> Minister that he should determine the matters outstanding from the referendums by the end of this month. He deliberately chose not to make a matching response but to try to manipulate the situation for his own ends. He can have no grounds for anger if others judge it for the manoeuvre that it was. Nor, in view of the government's conduct of parliamentary matters during the past three years, can he complain if his present action is dubbed characteristic.
>
> It is not unusual for minority governments to carry on for a considerable time, as this government have. What condemns the Prime Minister now is the justified feeling that the substance of matters before the House takes second place to the survival of the government. That feeling is widespread, and it robs the government and the Prime Minister of authority, credibility and dignity [a tricolon, or group of three]. The only way to renew the authority of parliamentary government is to seek a fresh mandate from the people and to seek it quickly. We challenge the government to do so before this day is through.

Thatcher's speech is partly effective because of *kairos* – the pivotal moment of high tension and knife-edge politics as one government dies and a new one is waiting to be born. It is also effective because of the way she fashions her arguments, marshals the points she wants to make and delivers them with trademark conviction. Take the section where Thatcher says that Labour has

> doubled prices, doubled dole queues, doubled debt,

> diminished our defences and undermined public respect and confidence in the law. There has been a failure not only of policies but of the whole philosophy on which they are based – the philosophy which elevates the state, dwarfs the individual and enlarges the bureaucracy. Across the western world, the tide is turning against that, and soon the same thing will happen here.

This is a neatly written encapsulation of her central argument that Labour had failed not because of some bad luck or mismanagement but because of a tragic flaw in its entire philosophy. This is good writing scaffolding a big idea, which is the formula for a great speech.

The Labour government lost the vote by one (311 to 310). The story of that night of high drama is told in James Graham's brilliant play *This House*.

No-confidence speech checklist

- This kind of speech is all about building a case for why a government should depart the stage (although the Cromwell quote is overused, so avoid it*)
- Use curated facts and figures, like a lawyer in court
- Choose the government's weak points and 'punch the bruise'

* On 20 April 1653, Oliver Cromwell told Parliament: 'It is not fit that you should sit here any longer. You have sat here too long for any good you have been doing lately. In the name of God, go.' In 1940, Leo Amery used a version of the quote in the Norway debate aimed at Chamberlain, and in 2022, David Davis said the same to Boris Johnson.

PAYING TRIBUTE TO A DEPARTED COLLEAGUE

A grand parliamentary tradition is to mark the death of a colleague with a series of speeches. When a notable person dies, especially an MP or former MP, the House will meet to eulogise their life. A eulogy is a speech delivered in praise of the departed person, usually highlighting their positive attributes through anecdote, humour or referring to something they said. To write a successful eulogy, you have to garner material about their life that is personal to the speaker. This might be the first time they met, some shared enterprise or endeavour, an acknowledgement of disagreement or falling out or the last time they saw them.

In the peroration of his eulogy to Sir David Amess, the Southend MP murdered in October 2021, Mark Francois MP says:

> Many members wish to pay tribute, so I will end with this: another thing about David was his legendary timekeeping, or rather lack of it. His constituency events always ran late because he was so popular and so many people wanted to speak to him.
>
> By the end of a busy constituency Friday, of which he had many, he was sometimes running up to an hour late – he invariably overran, and this afternoon, in his honour, so have I; sorry, Mr Speaker – but what better fault to have than that wonderful trait? Among some of his closest friends, he was known affectionately as the late Sir David Amess.
>
> Well, now he really is the late Sir David Amess. I am absolutely determined – I ask for the House's support in this

> – that he will not have died in vain. He is now resting in the arms of the God he worshipped devotedly his whole life, so farewell David, my colleague, my great friend – in fact, quite simply the best bloke I ever knew.

Francois's speech is filled with lovely stories about his political ally and friend, which earn him the right to this cheeky end. Note the rhetorical question about his 'wonderful trait' of lateness. However, the very end goes from the sonorous references to God, to the tricolon 'colleague', 'my great friend' and thirdly 'simply the best bloke I ever knew'. This last is an alliterative colloquialism, the use of informal or slang language.

Here's Prime Minister Boris Johnson speaking about the Birmingham MP Jack Dromey in his tribute in the House:

> Although Jack and I may have come from different political traditions, I knew him as a man of great warmth and energy and compassion. I can tell the House that one day – a very hot day – Jack was driving in Greece when he saw a family of British tourists, footsore, bedraggled and sunburned, with the children on the verge of mutiny against their father: an experience I understand. He stopped the car and invited them all in, even though there was barely any room. I will always be grateful for his kindness, because that father was me, and he drove us quite a long way.

You can hear Johnson's use of polysyndeton (the deliberate addition of conjunctions to separate the nouns) – 'warmth and energy and compassion' – in his tricolon, and then there is a second tricolon, 'footsore, bedraggled and sunburned'. The reveal at the end that the father was Johnson himself makes this a perfect anecdote – personally experienced and revealing of a deeper truth about the protagonist.

Jack Dromey's friend and colleague Liam Byrne MP gave the following eulogy:

> Jack Dromey was my mentor, my teacher, my political partner and my friend for almost a decade and a half in Birmingham [this opener is all about establishing the credentials, or the ethos, of the speaker]. Like for many of us here today he was like a father to me; indeed, he was at school with my dad, at Cardinal Vaughan in west London, part of that extraordinary generation of second-generation Irish kids: sharp, chippy, pushing [a neat tricolon], determined to make a contribution to social justice.
>
> It didn't always start smoothly: my godfather, Spud Murphy, then a prefect at Cardinal Vaughan, used to talk to me fondly about having to give Jack a clip round the ear for smoking behind the bike sheds at school. But Jack was not a rebel without a cause [an allusion to the 1955 James Dean movie]: his cause was social justice, and he fought for it his entire life. His glorious life was one long crusade for the underdog; he fought for them whenever and wherever he found them. His campaigns in Birmingham are innumerable: he fought for more police numbers, he fought for Covid families, he fought for the food bank, he fought for Erdington

High Street, he fought for manufacturing jobs, he fought for the factory at GKN – and this was all just in the last week of his life ['he fought' is repeated at the start of the sentence, a use of *anaphora*].

As you will know, Mr Speaker, Jack brought a particular approach to all his campaigns. It generally started with a very, very long list of bullet points, and Jack would start off by saying, 'Just three points,' and we would tease him as he got to, 'And seventeenthly,' but he brought to every single one of his campaigns what he used to fondly say was a certain '*je ne sais quoi*' [humour].

He made sure that at the core of every single one of his campaigns were the stories, because we have all been educated in the legend of Joe and Josephine Soap in the Dog and Duck in Erdington. He also brought to all his campaigns not just the art of coalition building but incredible calm, along with persistence. He used to very proudly say that his nickname in the union was 'Never snap, never flap Jack', and he reminded me of that very often as I was losing my rag over the past year and a half.

On the last day of Jack's life we were working together on a book about the future of our great region, the heart of Britain, and as ever he brought to that an extraordinary optimism. He put the green industrial revolution at the core of what he wrote, and this is what he wrote:

'I am passionate in my belief that change is possible. However, as my experience as an MP for a constituency with high levels of inequality and poverty, it is crucial that any change is not just ambitious in the objective of dealing with climate change, but radical in creating opportunity for all. There is much to do and little time to achieve it before it's too late.'

I say to the Mother of the House, my right hon. and learned friend the Member for Camberwell and Peckham [Ms Harman], and the family watching today, like you we have all struggled with the shock of loss. I myself have found comfort in the words not of an Irish poet but of a Greek, who wrote centuries ago:

'Even in our sleep, pain … falls drop by drop upon the heart, until, in our own despair, against our will, comes wisdom through the awful grace of God.' [An apposite quotation.]

The wisdom we draw from Jack Dromey's life is very simple: we should all try to be more Jack. Our community, our country, and this House of Commons [another tricolon] will be a damn sight better for that.

Tribute speech checklist

- Try to think of something highly personal and unique from your relationship with the departed colleague
- Speak of their good qualities
- Remember their family is listening
- It's not about you, it's about them
- Use anecdotes to bring the speech to life

AN APOLOGY

The first place MPs tend to apologise for misdemeanours these days is X, formerly known as Twitter. However, there is a parliamentary convention that MPs must apologise to the House of Commons if they have misbehaved.

Erskine May says that:

> The House is usually indulgent with regard to personal statements, and will permit personal explanations to be made without any question being before the House provided that the Speaker has been informed of what the member proposes to say, and has given leave. Because the practice of the House is not to permit such statements to be subject to intervention or debate, the precise contents of the proposed statement are submitted in advance to the Speaker to ensure that they are appropriate. Where the Independent Expert Panel requires an apology to be given by means of a personal statement, the text of the statement will also be agreed with the chair of the panel. The member granted the privilege of making such a statement may not therefore depart from the agreed text.

So for the writers, you must write a bomb-proof script, and for MPs, you must deliver it word-for-word or else. It is entirely for the Speaker to decide whether to take a personal statement or not.

Even the Speaker Lindsay Hoyle apologised in February 2024 after great fury over the way he had handled a debate on the Middle East:

> I have to say that I regret how it has ended up. It was not

> my intention. I wanted to ensure that all could express their views and all sides of the House could vote. As it was, in particular, the SNP was ultimately unable to vote on its proposition. I regret with sadness that it has ended up in this position. It was never my intention for it to end up like this. I was absolutely convinced that the decision was made with the right intentions. I recognise the strength of feeling of Members on this issue. It is clear that today has not shown the House at its best. I will reflect on my part in that, and of course I recommit myself to ensuring that all Members of this House are treated fairly.

If you have to apologise, the only way to do it is abjectly, sorrowfully, sincerely and fulsomely. A non-apology apology is worse than no apology. An MP might have to apologise to the House because they have been the subject of an investigation and report by the Committee on Standards, for disorderly conduct or for telling porkies in a debate. There's a pleasing spreadsheet of reasons why MPs have apologised to the House since 1979, including:

- Accusing another member of having been drinking (Nicholas Edwards)
- Saying rude things about Southern Region British Rail passengers (Peter Snape)
- Damaging the Speaker's chair (Dafydd Wigley)
- Allowing a party official into the civil servants' box (Kenneth Baker)

- Failing to declare an interest during a debate (Michael Portillo)
- Using unparliamentary language about Ben Bradshaw (George Galloway)
- Behaving poorly in the Strangers' Bar (Eric Joyce)

If you have to draft an apology, take it seriously. Do not make light of it. The House takes these things very seriously, even if you don't. You may feel unjustly treated and the whole thing is a storm in a teacup. Tough. You have to suck it up.

Here, Neil Coyle MP gets the tone and language completely right:

> I want to say how sorry I am for the upset and offence my behaviour caused last year. I wish to specifically apologise to the two complainants who were subject to my drunk and offensive behaviour and attitude. I cannot apologise enough for the harm and upset caused, and I am, frankly, ashamed of my conduct. It should not have happened. No one should leave any MP's company so shocked or appalled at their inappropriate behaviour or failure to meet the standards rightly expected of this office.
>
> I also apologise to my constituents in Southwark. They faithfully put their trust in me to stand up for their values here in Westminster in three consecutive general elections, and I failed to represent them in the way they deserve or a way they would recognise. I owe a debt of gratitude too large to ever repay to my constituents for the privilege of

> serving our wonderful, diverse community. I am ashamed that this apology is both necessary and overdue. I apologise to the members of my local Labour party, who also expect me to represent the best of our values in this place, and who last year I also let down so badly.

The heartfelt tone of the speech, and the sincerity that lay behind it, allowed this MP to rehabilitate their reputation, regain trust and win reselection and re-election. A half-hearted or disingenuous apology might well have had the opposite effect.

Apology speech checklist

- Make sure people believe you, or you'll be back having to do it again
- Lay your regret and remorse on with a trowel
- Keep it short and respectful
- Stick to the facts
- Make sure you do nothing that puts a bomb under your words (like smirking)

RESIGNATION SPEECH

This is when the MP is also a minister and is resigning from the government. Perhaps the most famous is Geoffrey Howe's in 1990, which presaged the defenestration of Margaret Thatcher with some bad-ass cricket metaphors.

Like a Maiden Speech, a resignation speech is heard in silence and without intervention. The most important aspect of a resignation speech, alongside the letter to the Prime Minister, is the central argument or rationale for the resignation. This is the minister's opportunity to place on record their own version of events for posterity.

In January 2022, government minister Lord Agnew decided to resign from the Boris Johnson government on the issue of the government's failure to tackle fraud and misuse of public funds. As he says himself with huge humility and self-effacement, Lord Agnew was a 'virtually unknown' minister; not even a household name in his own household. Yet his resignation captured the headlines and was judged as a noble act provoked by genuine morality. Nothing in his career became him like the leaving of it:

> Noble Lords can see that it is my deeply held conviction that the current state of affairs is not acceptable. Given that I am the minister for counter-fraud, it feels somewhat dishonest to stay on in that role if I am incapable of doing it properly, let alone of defending our track record. It is for this reason that I have, sadly, decided to tender my resignation as a minister across the Treasury and Cabinet Office with immediate effect. I would be grateful if my noble friend would pass this letter to the Prime Minister at his earliest convenience. It is worth saying that none of this relates to far more dramatic political events being played out across Westminster. This is not an attack on the Prime Minister, and I am sorry for the inconvenience it will cause. Indeed, I think any Prime Minister should be able to reasonably

expect that the levers of government are actually connected to delivering services for our citizens.

I hope that, as a virtually unknown minister beyond this place, giving up my career might prompt others more important than me to get behind this and sort it out. It matters for all the obvious reasons, but there is a penny of income tax waiting to be claimed here if we just woke up. Total fraud loss across government is estimated at £29 billion a year. Of course, not all can be stopped, but a combination of arrogance, indolence and ignorance freezes the government machine. Action taken today will give this government a sporting chance of cutting income tax before a likely May 2024 election. If my removal helps that to happen, it will have been worth it.

It leaves me only to thank the noble Lord, Lord Tunnicliffe, for his courteous but attentive role as shadow minister of my portfolio, and to thank noble friends, many of whom I know will carry on their scrutiny of this important area. Thank you, and goodbye.

And with that, Lord Agnew walked out of the House of Lords Chamber, in a calm and dignified manner, to enjoy his fifteen minutes of fame.

In March 2003, Robin Cook resigned from the Labour government because of his opposition to the prospect of war in Iraq. In his speech, Cook makes two direct appeals – one to the sense and wisdom of the British people, and the other to the importance of the House of Commons, which belies his twin intended audiences for this speech. In speechwriting, an appeal to the majority view of the people is called *argumentum ad populum*, or appeal to the people. The central theme of this, the peroration of the speech, is Cook's opposition to war.

Here is Cook's peroration:

> The longer that I have served in this place, the greater the respect I have for the good sense and collective wisdom of the British people. On Iraq, I believe that the prevailing mood of the British people is sound. They do not doubt that Saddam is a brutal dictator, but they are not persuaded that he is a clear and present danger to Britain. They want inspections to be given a chance, and they suspect that they are being pushed too quickly into conflict by a US Administration with an agenda of its own.
>
> Above all, they are uneasy at Britain going out on a limb on a military adventure without a broader international coalition and against the hostility of many of our traditional allies. From the start of the present crisis, I have insisted, as Leader of the House, on the right of this place to vote on whether Britain should go to war. It has been a favourite theme of commentators that this House no longer occupies a central role in British politics.
>
> Nothing could better demonstrate that they are wrong than for this House to stop the commitment of troops in a war that has neither international agreement nor domestic support. I intend to join those tomorrow night who will vote against military action now. It is for that reason, and

for that reason alone, and with a heavy heart, that I resign from the government.

This is considered by many to be a dignified, prescient and principled resignation from Cabinet. How does he achieve it? Cook had a reputation as a forensic, detailed parliamentary debater. His finest moment was his performance in Parliament in response to the Scott Report into the arms-to-Iraq scandal in 1996. Cook had two hours to read the five-volume, 2000-page report before appearing in Parliament, and yet he delivered a devastating, excoriating speech. In his resignation speech, Cook showed this lawyerly, considered trait. His resignation was delivered in sorrow not anger, with calmness not invective. He makes his assertion, using a contrasting pair, that war in Iraq has 'neither international agreement nor domestic support'. He appealed to the common sense of the British people, rather than arcane points of law. But his main appeal, aimed squarely at those listening in the Chamber, was that Parliament itself had the chance to do something important to alter the course of events. Robin Cook's resignation from government was subsidiary to his opposition to the war.

Resignation speech checklist

- Offer up to history the reasons for your departure, as your enemies will be putting around their own versions of events
- Remain calm and dignified at all times
- Be deferential to Parliament and the Chamber, as this is the first audience you have to win over

- Use a stiletto not a sledgehammer
- Think Geoffrey Howe

VALEDICTORY SPEECH – SAYING GOODBYE TO THE GASWORKS

Eventually, every MP makes their last speech in the Chamber. If there's any kind of planning involved in their departure, they will get a chance to make a valedictory, or farewell, speech. At the end of each parliament, many members will retire and say goodbye to the old place, although some will reappear in ermine at the other end of the building.

For example, on 24 May 2024, the 'valedictory debate' took place in the Commons, just ahead of the 2024 general election. Speakers included Harriet Harman, Theresa May, Barry Sheerman, Ben Wallace, Ian Blackford, Margaret Hodge, Matt Hancock, Robert Halfon, Julian Knight, Bob Stewart, Jo Churchill, Alok Sharma, Tracey Crouch, Andrew Percy, Nickie Aiken, Robert Neill, David Jones, Stephen Hammond, Tim Loughton, Mark Menzies, Robin Walker, Dehenna Davison, Will Quince, James Duddridge, John Baron, Steve Brine, Andy Carter, Greg Clark, Richard Bacon and Matthew Offord, representing several hundred years of parliamentary experience.

The tone of a valedictory speech is non-partisan, anecdotal, respectful and, if possible, self-effacing. The valedictory debate is an example of a parliamentary moment. It's a bit of a love-in. This convivial atmosphere was helped along by the Deputy Speaker Nigel Evans's responses to the speeches:

'We will miss you like mad, too. We love you.'

'Thank you, Robert, we will miss you.'

'I love you, Bob.'

'Thank you, Tracey. I love you.'

'You are a true friend, Andy… Love you loads.'

I'm not sure what Erskine May would have made of that. Evans never made his own valedictory speech. His 18,000 majority was overturned in the 2024 Labour landslide and he lost his seat.

Gordon Brown's valedictory speech in March 2015 is a good example of how to do it:

> It is important that I start today by thanking you:
>
> Mr Speaker, for your leadership in this House, your dedication to our parliamentary democracy and your unfailing courtesy to all sides.
>
> Let me also thank the staff of this House – from the clerks, cleaners and catering staff to the librarians and doorkeepers – for their non-partisan and always unselfish support.
>
> And thank my colleagues on this side – so many so brilliant to work alongside – whose wisdom and friendship have sustained my family in times of personal loss.
>
> And let me thank colleagues on all sides, especially all those who leave the House today. Let me thank all for their outstanding contribution to what we are right to believe is the greatest democracy in the world.
>
> Most of all, I owe a debt of gratitude to my constituents, who sent me here and accorded me the privilege of trust

and service over thirty-two years, in which time I have always tried to speak up for their concerns and aspirations.

When I stood for Parliament in 1983, I asked my constituents to elect me as a candidate of youth and fresh ideas. Of course, by 2010, I had to change tack: I asked them to elect me as the candidate of maturity and experience!

But when I first arrived here in 1983 I was so unknown, so patently here just to make up the numbers and so clearly forgettable that *The Times* newspaper confused me with one of the many other Browns in Parliament – there were as many MPs named Brown as there were SDP or Liberal MPs – and published a photo of me when I was a student alongside a caption that said that I was born in 1926. In quick succession, each London newspaper repeated this error – not so much the power of the press as the power of the press cutting – labelling me successively as 'elderly', 'a veteran' and 'an old Labour stalwart' – definitely old Labour – with the result that a few days later, I received a note from a pension company to the effect that I had entered a new job late in life and would want to make provision for an early retirement.

It is for others to judge what has been achieved between then and now. But today it is not my constituency, not Scotland and not public service that I am leaving: it is Westminster and London I leave to live full time in the place where I grew up and where my children will grow up and complete their schooling – and it is my good fortune that Fife has not only been my constituency for a third of a century, but always my home.

I leave this House feeling a huge amount of gratitude – but also with some concern. For I sense that the UK today is fragile, at risk and we are potentially at a point of departure.

Countries at their best, their strongest, their truest, are more than places on the map, more than a demarcation of borders. Great countries stand on shared foundations. They are guided by unifying ideals. They move forward in common purpose. And so it must be with Britain.

And whether the future lies in greater devolution, a new form of federalism or home rule within the UK, in the constitutional revolution now under way I will fight, struggle, do battle and fight and fight again to renew and reconstruct for a new age the idea of Britain around shared values that can bring us together and advance a common Britishness – a shared belief in tolerance, liberty and fairness that come alive in unique British institutions like the National Health Service and in common policies for social justice – ideas that we have given to the world but now seem to be losing sight of at home: unifying ideas that we need to champion anew at the core of a common British national purpose that binds us together in a shared future.

It is because I believe in Britain's future that I am saddened – and I am sorry to have to say this – that for the first and only time in 300 years since the start of the Union, it has become official UK government policy to create two classes of elected representatives – 'first class' English who would vote on all issues, and 'second class' Scots who would vote on only some – and thus to mimic the nationalists by driving a wedge between Scotland and England – and this only to head off opposition from the extremes with a direct nationalist appeal to the English electorate … Not so much 'English votes for English laws' as 'English laws for English votes.'

But I ask this House to remember that our greatest successes as a country have come not when we have been divided nor when we have turned inwards, but when we have confidently looked outwards and thought globally, our eyes fixed on the wider world and the future.

With the unwinding of the Pax Americana, and in the wake of the recent retreat from global co-operation – for today we have no global climate change treaty, no global financial standards and for the first time in half a century no world trade agreement – we must recapture what now seems a distant memory – the heightened global co-ordination of 2009 which Britain led – and never allow ourselves to become spectators or watchers on the shore, when the world needs us, in Europe and beyond, to lead and champion global action to deal with poverty, pollution, proliferation and protectionism – and to defuse what is potentially the biggest global flashpoint: the growing anger of millions of disenfranchised young people in the poorest countries at the unacceptable denial of the basic opportunities they deserve and demand. And so it is right and it is a tribute to all here that two of the last Acts of this parliament are new laws on aid and slavery, guaranteeing the British people's long-term support to the most vulnerable in the world.

And it is more than economics. Over thirty years I, like most on both sides of this House, have condemned the discrimination and the prejudices of the past which should now be consigned forever to that past. And like many I have welcomed – indeed have been a cheerleader for – the new freedoms and the new rights, the equality and anti-discrimination laws, that we have enacted and embraced not as a departure from our longstanding values of tolerance, liberty and fairness but as the modern realisation of them. These include not just changes in the law but also symbolic expressions of a changed Britain – the Mandela, Gandhi and soon Emily Davidson statues here, the Turing apology and the apology to child migrants, which together write a new chapter in our country's history.

All societies need a moral energy that can inspire individuals to the self-sacrificial acts of public service that come alive out of mutual respect and obligation, and can turn impersonal buildings and anonymous streets made only of stone and concrete into vibrant, sharing communities.

Yes, the predominant feeling in our country today is an anger I can see in people's faces and hear in their voices – an anger directed against elites – and a demand for change.

Yes, too, of the many social changes that I have witnessed in thirty years here, among the most dramatic has been the significant fall in religious observance.

But I also sense that the British people are better than

leaders often presume; ready to respond to a vision of a country more caring and less selfish, more compassionate and less cynical than any 'me too, me first, me now, me above all, me whatever' manifestos.

For I sense millions of us feel, however distantly, the pain of others and believe in something within ourselves, beyond ourselves and bigger than ourselves that can lead us to work for causes greater than ourselves. And so we cannot easily feast when our fellow citizens go hungry to food banks; we cannot feel at ease when our neighbours – in hock to payday lenders – are ill at ease; and cannot be fully content when, with poverty pay and zero-hour contracts, there is around us so much discontent.

And so I repeat: it's not anti-wealth to say that the wealthy must do more to lift up those who are not wealthy. It's not anti-enterprise to say the enterprising must do more to meet the aspirations of those who have never had the chances to show that they too are enterprising. And it's not anti-market to say that markets need morals to underpin their success.

And for me, the most moving mission statement defining our duties as MPs here is the declaration made nearly 100 years ago – on the day after they were elected – by MPs from Clydeside, that we should 'abjure vanity and self-aggrandisement' and, as 'humble servants of the people', 'have regard for the weak, those stricken by disease, those who have fallen in the struggle for life' and 'bear in our hearts the sorrows of the aged, the widowed mother, and the poor, that their lives shall not be without comfort.'

And for this – and for showing me that when the strong help the weak it makes us all stronger – I will always be grateful to my parents who taught me these values of justice, my party who taught me how to fight for justice, and my constituents who taught me every day the rightness of justice.

For we must never forget that what politics at its best can do is imbue people with hope and inspire us all to be better.

Wishful thinking about the future is the passive belief something might be done.

Optimism is the instinctive belief that yes, something can be done.

But hope is the active resolve that something must be done.

When in 1886 Tennyson wrote one of his last poems, 'Locksley Hall – Sixty Years After', with its pessimistic refrain 'Chaos, Cosmos! Cosmos, Chaos! Who can tell how all will end!', the then Prime Minister Gladstone was moved to remind Tennyson that in his first famous 'Locksley Hall' poem six decades before he had, and I cite, 'dipt into the future far as human eye could see; Saw the Vision of the world, and all the wonder that would be.'

I have spoken today of what endures beyond anyone's time in office, and thinking beyond the perils of things as they are to the wonders of things as they could be – and with hope unbroken, idealism unbowed, a desire to serve undiminished – I leave here as I came here, with an unquenchable faith in a future for our country that we can build and share together, a future where we help shape the

> world beyond our shores, a future where we always demand the best of ourselves. This is the future worth fighting for and this is the future that I will never stop fighting for.

This speech contains the right blend of deference to the House, self-effacing humour and anecdote, national and global scope, and a clear through-line of progressive values. He mentions the Red Clydesiders, Mandela, Gandhi and Emily Davison.

It casts itself forward not back and ends with energy and defiance. It is the speech of someone not only reminiscing but also thinking ahead to what comes next. This is what the line 'the future that I will never stop fighting for' signals.

Earlier, we saw how Margaret Thatcher encapsulated her credo into a few highly economical lines. Brown does the same in this speech:

> It's not anti-wealth to say that the wealthy must do more to lift up those who are not wealthy. It's not anti-enterprise to say the enterprising must do more to meet the aspirations of those who have never had the chances to show that they too are enterprising. And it's not anti-market to say that markets need morals to underpin their success.

This is an expression of Brown's social-democratic philosophy in just a few well-chosen words. You can see how it falls into three parts (and three is the magic number) and uses anaphoric repetition of 'anti' to reinforce the point. This is more than pleasing word-play; it is language in the service of ideas.

Valedictory speech checklist

- It's an intensely personal moment, so choose the right stories about your parliamentary career to be on the record
- Try to raise a laugh or two with some funny stories, especially if the joke is about you
- Be nice to the House staff and the Speaker
- Say generous things about your colleagues
- Bow out with grace

In this chapter, we have seen that there are different types of parliamentary speeches, each reflecting the purpose and function of Parliament itself. Some are about holding the executive to account. Some are about representing a constituency. Some are about making better laws. Some are about representing the nation, or some great section of it, in moments of triumph, trial or tribulation. Some are about the customs of the House. The writer and MP must be across these forms, and they will need to tailor the tone, length and language of their speech to the occasion.

Yet we have also seen there are unifying themes. You must always deploy language in service of the big purpose of the speech. Without a clear idea of 'why' rather than 'what', the speech is doomed. The speaker must always have an eye on the audiences, both in the Chamber, back in the constituency and more widely across social media. The speech must be well-honed and edited, remembering that simplicity is the greatest virtue in speechwriting and longevity is the greatest vice. And finally, the member must deliver it with conviction and all of the skills of an actor, stand-up, lawyer and salesperson combined.

CHAPTER FOUR

THE ART OF RHETORIC

So much has been written about rhetoric since Aristotle was in short trousers, but in essence, rhetoric is using language to persuade, delight, entertain, inform and enhance the reputation of the speaker. It is simply about putting words in certain forms and saying them out loud. When I write a speech for an MP, I stress they are all their own words; I've just put them in the right place. Despite the advent of social media, our shortening attention spans and a general lack of interest in parliamentary debate, there is a huge role, necessity even, for rhetoric in Parliament. Without it, we may as well shut down the Chamber and set up a massive WhatsApp group.

The Greeks and Romans, when not empire-building, conquering or enslaving, spent a lot of their time thinking about their language. The Ancients' gift to us all is rhetoric, or using words to delight, stir and persuade. These days, the term 'rhetorical' suggests empty phrases and hot air. 'Mere rhetoric' is almost an insult, as though rhetoric was the opposite of substance. We are going to use the term rhetoric in its proper sense: of words that work.

Rhetorical devices are used in literature, popular culture and our conversations. *You Talkin' to Me? Rhetoric from Aristotle to Obama* is the title of Sam Leith's excellent book on the subject. It's taken from the movie *Taxi Driver*, and it's a rhetorical question. We hear and use rhetorical devices without necessarily knowing what they're called, in the same way you can listen to music without knowing your aria from your elegy.

The ancient Greeks and Romans devoted huge amounts of time and effort to developing styles of persuasion using language and giving them names: *apodioxis*, *chiasmus*, *diazeugma*, *metanoia*, *paralipsis*, *polyptoton*, *systrophe*, *tmesis* and about a million others (hyperbole). Once you get past the funny-sounding names, you can identify ways of speaking and writing that may well be familiar and commonplace:

'Nice weekend?' 'Yeah, not bad.' (*Litotes*) 'You?'

'Nah, Worst. Night. Ever.' (Hyperbolic asyndetic tricolon)

'Bit of a bender?' (Alliteration)

'Abso-bloody-lutely.' (*Tmesis*)

Rhetoric and rhetorical devices surround us like oxygen – in movies and television, in advertising, in magazines and in the words we read, write and speak.

In *You Talkin' to Me?* Sam Leith writes:

> Rhetoric is language at play; language plus. It is what persuades and cajoles, inspires and bamboozles, thrills and misdirects. It causes criminals to be convicted and then frees those criminals on appeal. It causes governments to rise and fall, best men to be ever shunned by their friend's

> brides and perfectly sensible adults to march with steady purpose towards machine guns.

Leith is right – rhetoric is the ability to persuade (for good or ill). But he also makes the important point that rhetoric is language at play. One of the best things about being a speechwriter is the fun. We do it for the larks. It may not seem like it, faced with a blank screen, a blanker mind, a badgering Member of Parliament and a looming deadline, but speechwriting should be the moment of the week when you are most stimulated, most skilful, most creative. Honestly, it can be great fun.

A love of language helps. Writers are readers. Writers are lovers of words. George Orwell in *Why I Write* describes his discovery, aged sixteen, of 'the joy of mere words, i.e. the sounds and associations of words'. Note Orwell's use of 'joy' and also 'sounds'. Speechwriters tend to enjoy music, poetry, wordplay, stand-up comedy and theatre, and a good speech contains elements of each. Lest we are accused of Eurocentrism, we should note that every civilisation and language has forms of words designed to persuade, inform and delight. Humans have always wanted to persuade other humans to think things and do stuff, and always will. I once heard a speech by Anne Makinda, the veteran Tanzanian politician, in Tanzania. She addressed the audience in Swahili. Even though my Swahili extends only as far as 'safari' and 'jambo' I could identify rhetorical devices in her words and observe how they roused her audience. For example, she used groups of three, alliteration, cacophony, and varied the tempo and volume of her speech to great effect.

It has always struck me that rhetoric is the one discipline that has not really developed from the days of the ancient Romans. The others, whether medicine, law, engineering, agriculture, architecture, maths, physics, chemistry or whatever, have developed and improved down the centuries. The Greeks and the Romans nailed it three thousand years ago, and we haven't really improved on it since. If Cicero landed up in the public gallery of the House of Commons, he would recognise many of the techniques he used in his great speeches.

Some parliamentarians have been taught rhetoric at school or university and consciously use it in their speeches. Boris Johnson is perhaps the best modern example. In the past, the dominance of MPs from public schools meant that many had a 'classical education' and had absorbed the tropes of classical rhetoric, consciously or not. It is not unreasonable to assume that Sir Robert Uniacke-Penrose-Fitzgerald, 1st Baronet of Lisquinlan and Corkbeg, or Captain The Honourable Seymour Fitzroy Ormsby-Gore had a smattering of Latin.

Henry Brougham MP (1778–1868) holds the record for the longest-ever parliamentary speech (over six hours). He had studied rhetoric at Edinburgh University and wrote well-received essays on Demosthenes.

William Gladstone opened his speech defending atheist Liberal MP Charles Bradlaugh, in April 1883, with this:

> Many members of this House will recollect, perhaps, the noble and majestic lines – for such they are – of the Latin poet:

omnis enim per se divum natura necessest
immortali aevo summa cum pace fruatur
semota ab nostris rebus seiunctaque longe;
nam privata dolore omni, privata periclis,
ipsa suis pollens opibus, nihil indiga nostri,
nec bene promeritis capitur nec tangitur ira.

Gladstone neither bothers to tell the House that the 'Latin poet' is Lucretius, assuming most will know, nor to translate the lines into English, assuming there is no need. I've just read out and timed this quote in my best Gladstonian tones, and it takes about forty-five seconds. Imagine anything like this in today's Parliament!

For most of the eighteenth and nineteenth centuries, statesmen would fire Latin and Greek quotations at each other across the chamber, like the salvos from a naval frigate.

Others such as Winston Churchill were taught to recite verse by heart, with the rhythms and cadence of poetry entering their bones. Churchill won a prize at Harrow for memorising and declaiming Macaulay's *Lays of Ancient Rome*, including the famous lines that appear on his lips in the film *Darkest Hour* (yes, I know the scene on the District line is entirely fictitious and rather silly):

Then out spake brave Horatius,
The Captain of the Gate:
'To every man upon this earth
Death cometh soon or late.

And how can man die better
Than facing fearful odds,
For the ashes of his fathers,
And the temples of his Gods.'

Churchill wrote in *My Early Life*:

> By being so long in the lowest form [at Harrow] I gained an immense advantage over the cleverer boys … I got into my bones the essential structure of the ordinary British sentence – which is a noble thing … Naturally I am biased in favour of boys learning English; I would make them all learn English: and then I would let the clever ones learn Latin as an honour, and Greek as a treat.

In our own times, the place many MPs learned their rhetoric was at university, and especially the Oxford Union, the Cambridge Union and the debating societies of other top universities.

That is not to say the art of rhetoric was the sole preserve of the public-school boys and university graduates. Folk such as Angela Rayner learned their debating skills in a very different kind of union, in her case, Unison. Those Radical, Liberal and later Labour MPs who did not attend Eton or Harrow were no less well-versed. They learned to speak with passion and verve in the pulpit, on the street corner, standing on soap boxes, in outdoor meetings, in works canteens and trade union meetings.

For example, Ian Mikardo describes the 'open-air university' of Mile End Waste in the East End of London before the war, where Jewish East Enders would gather in dozens of *dredles* or circles of intense debate and discussion 'with participants and listeners often moving from one to the other, ever seeking a livelier discussion than the one before. I did exactly that, and it was the greatest pleasure of the week; and after a while I became one of the debaters rather than a mere auditor.'

Barbara Castle recalls that her role as a local Labour Party 'propaganda secretary', in which she was required to carry a wooden rostrum to the Hyde market square every Saturday night and often speak herself when the guest speaker failed to show up, was 'the most rigorous training in public speaking that any politician could hope for'.

This kind of street-corner training seems to have disappeared from our public life, with candidates and MPs under threat of assault, or worse, in public spaces. The last hurrah was perhaps John Major, thirty years ago. John Major had learned the craft of public debate on a soap box in Brixton market in the late 1960s, where he would engage in what he called 'badinage' with the locals. It was quite normal for those seeking office to stand on a box and engage the voters. Now, it would be seen as somewhat eccentric and certainly dangerous to their safety.

Whether trained at the Oxford Union, or the Union of Mineworkers, MPs have been using rhetorical devices since Parliament was first summoned. Some have done so consciously, based on their studies of the classics. Others have done so through trial and error, honing their craft in car parks and canteens, like the old club comedians at the Glasgow Empire.

Google it, and you will find long lists of rhetorical devices, most with funny-sounding Greek names. Every book on speechwriting contains lists of them. Some are obscure. Some are commonplace, like anecdote, or the telling of stories, or alliteration whereby the words start with the same sounds. Many are used every day in Parliament, without the MP or their staff knowing what they are called or that they even are rhetorical devices.

A quick sidebar. Rhetorical devices in a speech are designed to sound good, not read well. Speechwriting is more about the musicality of the words than writing a policy brief. Consider this final line of Henry Brougham's speech in October 1831 in support of the Reform Bill:

'By all you hold most dear, by all the ties that bind every one of us to our common order and our common country, I solemnly abjure you. I warn you. I implore you, yea on my bended knees I supplicate you – reject not this bill!'

Read this on the page, and now read it out loud. You can hear the rhythm, the metre, the drumbeat, the music. It is always a good idea to read out what you've written in a speech to hear what it sounds like when freed in the air, not locked in the ink.

The trick here is to select the rhetorical devices that work best for you in Parliament and make them your own. To get started, just select a few and try them out. Then select a few more and stretch your legs a little. You might start with a checklist and tick them off. Soon, they start to flow effortlessly. There are loads, but some of the main ones we will explore in this chapter are: tricolons, rhetorical questions, alliteration, allusion, anecdote, quotation, euphemism, imagery, repetition, metaphor and humour.

These rhetorical devices are our friends. So, in honour of all those episodes of *Friends* entitled 'The One…' here are my top ten rhetorical devices to pep up your speeches.

TRICOLON: THE ONE THAT COMES IN THREES, TRIOS AND TRIPLETS

Perhaps the most famous rhetorical trick is to put things in threes. You hear this called the power of three, the rule of three, trebling, trios or its proper name tricolon.

It could be three words or three phrases, or three words the same, or two words and a longer third part. The Romans said *omne trium perfectum* – everything in a three is perfect, and they weren't wrong. There is something deeply satisfying about threes. Like a three-legged stool, they stand up without wobbling.

They appear across our culture: three witches, three wise monkeys, three blind mice, three wise men, three musketeers, three men in a boat, three little pigs, Goldilocks and the three bears and on and on and on. This principle has been applied to popular sayings, political slogans, advertising, titles, and memorable lines in speeches. They are ingrained into our culture and hard-wired into our brains. Three is a magic number, and not just in Kabbalah.

Once you start to list them out, from all the different

continents, centuries and languages, you realise they come in multiple forms. They don't exist solely in English, or even European languages, but appear in every tongue. The Iranian revolution was founded on the principle *Estiqlal, Azadi, Jomhuri-ye Eslami* (Independence, Freedom, Islamic Republic). Swahili speakers reckon that *uvumilivu, pambano na bidii ndizo zinazochangia sana kwa mafanikio* ('patience, persistence and perspiration make an unbeatable combination for success').

Comedians use them all the time, usually with the third part a discordant twist on the first two. You set up a pattern, then break it. When *Watership Down* was in the cinemas, an enterprising local butcher put a sign in his shop window: 'You've read the book, you've seen the film, now eat the characters.'

Can you name the sources of these?

- Ready, steady, go!
- Hands, Face, Space
- The good, the bad and the ugly
- Ready, aim, fire!
- Rock, paper, scissors
- Education, Education, Education
- Stay at Home, Protect the NHS, Save Lives
- See it, say it, sorted
- Beanz Meanz Heinz
- Snap! Crackle! Pop!
- Friends, Romans, Countrymen
- Veni, Vidi, Vici
- *Ethos, pathos, logos*

- Lights, cameras, action
- Liberté, Égalité, Fraternité
- Government of the people, by the people, for the people
- Father, Son and Holy Ghost
- A Mars a day helps you work, rest and play
- Wine, women and song
- Sex, drugs and rock 'n' roll
- Life, Liberty, and the Pursuit of Happiness

Examples from parliamentary speeches abound. For example, in Tony Blair's final speech as Prime Minister, he said of David Cameron, then Leader of the Opposition, that he had been 'most proper, correct and courteous in his dealings with me'.

In opposing Labour's constitutional reforms in 1997, William Hague asked:

'What is the logic, the principle or the deep constitutional thinking that leads the government to treat Scotland and Wales in such radically different ways?'

Here's Margaret Thatcher's famous riposte to Jacques Delors in 1990:

> The President of the Commission, Mr Delors, said at a press conference the other day that he wanted the European Parliament to be the democratic body of the Community, he wanted the Commission to be the Executive and he wanted the Council of Ministers to be the Senate. No. No. No.

The last bit is the famous use of a tricolon, in this case epizeuxis meaning the same word repeated for emphasis, but note the preceding sentence is also a tricolon, with 'he wanted' repeated at the start. This is *anaphora*. By contrast, Labour leader Michael Foot, speaking in the debate on the invasion of the Falklands in 1982, said, 'We have a moral duty, a political duty and every other kind of duty…' This repetition of 'duty' at the end of the phrase is called *epistrophe*.

Here's Labour MP Arthur Greenwood in the Norway debate in 1940, when the government's calamitous handling of the opening stages of the Second World War was under assault: 'It is perfectly clear that there must be an active, vigorous, imaginative direction of the war.' By missing out the (grammatically correct) 'and' before the word 'imaginative', Greenwood is using *asyndeton*, meaning deliberately leaving out the conjunctions for greater impact.

In the same debate, Liberal giant Lloyd George described the dire situation as 'a great national, imperial and world issue'. This one is interesting because it is a *tricolon crescens*, or ascending tricolon, with each part larger than the last – nation, then empire, then world. The opposite is a *tricolon diminuens*, or descending tricolon.

Tony Blair's famous tricolon 'Education, Education, Education' is usually written up as a use of *asyndeton* (with the 'and' missing) but his actual delivery at the Labour Party conference in 1996 includes the 'and' in the grammatically correct place.

Tricolons do not have to be short and snappy. More languorous phraseology will work just as well. Tessa Jowell told the House in January 2005, 'In this country we have a severe problem with drink, drink-related crime and behaviour that is associated with people getting drunk.' Later in the same speech, she said, 'The answer to the problems that we have lies in local democracy, a more responsible drink industry and police with the power to take on the yobs.' You can see that tricolons don't have to be concise.

But they do have to be in threes. You can use balanced couplets, or lists, but nothing is as effective as things in threes. Unlike many of the other rhetorical devices, which should be used sparingly, you can pile in loads of tricolons and the Chamber will lap 'em up.

Tricolon checklist

- The human brain loves things in threes; it's the magic number
- Tricolons pop up across the centuries, in every language, on every continent
- You can vary them: three words, three sentences, two short words and a long sentence, the same word repeated
- You can use this one multiple times in a speech; Barack Obama uses them on every page

RHETORICAL QUESTION: ISN'T THAT THE ONE WHERE YOU ASK A QUESTION?

Yes, it is. It's a question that does have an answer, but the answer comes in the mind of a listener. The idea of a rhetorical question is to plant a thought in the heads of the listeners. Political examples include Edward Heath's question to the electorate in 1974 of 'who governs?' which was answered with 'not you, mate', or Ronald Reagan's famous question in the debate with President Carter in 1980, 'Are you better off today than you were four years ago?' This last one has reappeared in political debates ever since.

Here's Tony Benn MP in 1998, in a debate about bombing Saddam Hussein's forces in Iraq:

> I was in London in the Blitz in 1940, living in the Millbank Tower, where I was born. Some different ideas have come in since. Every night, I went down to the shelter in Thames House. Every morning, I saw dockland burning. Five hundred people were killed in Westminster one night by a land mine. It was terrifying. Aren't Arabs? Aren't Iraqis terrified? Don't Arab and Iraqi women weep when their children die? Doesn't bombing strengthen their determination? What fools we are to live in a generation to which war is a computer game for our children and just an interesting little Channel 4 news item.

More recently, Keir Starmer said this at the Despatch Box:

'Do not the British people deserve a Prime Minister they can trust, not a government who are mired in sleaze, cronyism and scandal?'

This was Prime Minister's Questions (PMQs) so it had to be framed as a question, but it remains a rhetorical question nonetheless. Also note the neat tricolon 'sleaze, cronyism and scandal'.

Note that a rhetorical question is not the same as a question with an actual answer. If you pose a question in a speech that you then answer yourself, it's called *hypophora*. For example, Winston Churchill's famous 'blood, toil, tears and sweat' speech in the House of Commons on 13 May 1940:

> You ask, what is our policy? I will say: It is to wage war, by sea, land and air, with all our might and with all the strength that God can give us; to wage war against a monstrous tyranny, never surpassed in the dark and lamentable catalogue of human crime. That is our policy. You ask, what is our aim? I can answer in one word: Victory. Victory at all costs – Victory in spite of all terror – Victory, however long and hard the road may be, for without victory there is no survival.

Lynne Truss in her *Eats, Shoots and Leaves* tells us tantalisingly that in the 1580s, a typesetter called Henry Dunham invented the rhetorical question mark. It was the same as the question mark we know and love (?) but pointing away from the end of the sentence, not towards it. Alas, it has fallen into disuse.

Rhetorical questions can be a useful tool in the toolkit, as long as the answer is the one you want. This comes down to knowing your audience, understanding their concerns and instincts and calibrating the rhetorical question towards the answer you know (or hope) they will come up with.

As with all great speeches, the speaker needs to know their audience, and when it goes wrong, it is because speaker and audience are out of sync. This is always the speaker's fault, never the audience's.

Rhetorical questions checklist

- This is a device for planting a thought into the mind of the listener
- It can work well at the end of a speech
- Be clear what the answer to your question is

ALLITERATION: THE ONE WHERE THE WORDS WORK WELL WITH ONE ANOTHER

You'll have likely done this one at school. 'Peter Piper picked a peck of pickled peppers,' or some such. It is much-loved by poets, songwriters, Fleet Street headline writers and speechwriters. Alliteration is the repetition of consonant sounds at the start of, or sometimes within, words. The word comes from *littera*, the Latin word for 'letter'.

An example is the Labour slogan in 2010, 'A Future Fair for All'. Some people were disappointed that there wasn't an actual fair, with bumper cars and goldfish in bags. Or the Plaid Cymru slogan 'Working for Wales', or generic slogans such as 'power to the people', 'black is beautiful', 'the personal is political' or Theresa May's 'strong and stable'.

Here's Michael Gove in April 2024: 'The thousands of jobs created in Teesworks stand in stark contrast to Labour's failure, from London to Liverpool, to bring in the jobs required.' London and Liverpool could have been Brighton to Manchester, but it simply wouldn't have sounded as good.

This is Denis Healey dismissing a speech by his Conservative opponent in 1978 as being no more than a 'tedious and tendentious farrago of moth-eaten cuttings presented to him by the Conservative Research Department'. The double 't' sound works well. Healey could even have swapped out Conservative for 'Tory' and 'presented to him' for 'taken from' and had a running 't' sound through the sentence.

For example, William Hague in July 2000 complained about 'spin doctors and soundbites'. The obvious alliteration is at the start of 'spin' and 'soundbites' but also at the end of 'doctors' and 'soundbites', giving us four of the same sound. This use of the 's' sound specifically is called sibilance.

In his speech marking the retirement of Speaker of the House Betty Boothroyd, Tony Benn said, 'In addition, Madam Speaker, you have interpreted democracy not in terms of directives from above and discipline, but in terms of the debate, diversity, disagreement and decision that are the mainspring of a democratic Parliament.'

The trick to alliteration is to use it sparingly. Imagine if Tony Benn had continued his speech with 'dirty, disgraceful, disreputable, disputatious, downright deadly Daffy Duck'. Too much, Tony, too much.

If alliteration was a foodstuff, it would be a spice such as cardamon or cloves. A little bit can be delicious, but too much can overpower the dish. Cicero warned against the overuse of alliteration, and as ever, he was correct. It is a device that works best when used sparingly. If your speech is over-peppered with alliterative sounds, it will start to sound like Dylan Thomas, or worse, a children's tongue twister.

Alliteration is definitely worth trying for size. It shows that the writer has thought about the words and honed them into shape. An audience appreciates the effort. It displays thought and application.

The newly elected MP for Huntingdon, Ben Obese-Jecty, made a clever alliteration-related joke in his Maiden Speech: 'From the market towns of Huntingdon and St Ives to our rural villages, from Sawtry to Somersham, Houghton to Hamerton, Covington to Colne and Pidley to Perry – and three dozen others that will not stretch to my tortured alliteration – each has their own character and identity.'

He makes a good, self-effacing joke but highlights too the dangers of too much alliteration spoiling the effect. Perhaps once or twice in a speech, but no more. Alliteration always allows the audience to appreciate the argument, but a multiplicity mangles the meaning.

Alliteration checklist

- Alliteration is a neat device to show you've thought about the words you're uttering
- It's pleasing to the ear (and fun to say)
- It should be used sparingly, like cardamon or cinnamon

ALLUSION: THE ONE WHERE YOU REFER TO A SOURCE, FOR EXAMPLE A BOOK, PLAY OR FILM

Allusion is a reference in a speech to a notable work. It could be a poem, play, novel, song or other artistic endeavour, including other people's speeches (or even your own, you bighead). Unlike in academia, you are under no obligation to cite the source of your allusion or even mention the original work on which it is based. You can just drop it in and see if anyone recognises it. Allusion is a chance to show a bit of knowledge and make some connection with the audience, but the danger is that the reference is lost.

The MP is almost certainly well-educated and well-read and could dip into a store of knowledge to allude in their speeches. But remember, you don't want to use allusions that are too highbrow or obscure. You're not T. S. Eliot. This, however, didn't stop Boris Johnson dipping endlessly into the classics for his allusions.

On the other hand, allusions to pop culture (Beyoncé, *Traitors*, *Love Island*, Wireless festival) might sound horribly fake in the mouths of most MPs. You also have to be careful of alluding to things that make you sound old and out-of-touch, like the *Goons*, or *Dad's Army* (or *Friends* – ed.).

In December 1945, on a motion seeking to censure the Labour government, Prime Minister Clement Attlee accuses Winston Churchill of going down 'the primrose path, which, everybody remembers, leads to the eternal bonfire'.

Do they? It's an allusion to *Hamlet*, but I'm not sure everyone in the Chamber would have got that, and Shakespeare says nothing about eternal bonfires, so perhaps Attlee hadn't quite remembered it either.

Here's Aneurin Bevan fulminating against the introduction of charges into the NHS in 1951: 'The health service will be like Lavinia – all the limbs cut off and eventually her tongue cut out too.' Here, he's referencing *Titus Andronicus*, one of Shakespeare's lesser-known plays. Would his audience know that?

As well as Shakespeare, the other traditional go-to for allusion is the Bible. Today, Parliament is a far more multi-faith institution, but many twentieth-century parliamentarians were schooled in the Bible and represented a more Bible-literate population. When Margaret Thatcher says, 'The Jeremiahs sometimes say that the ordinary people of this country have lost the will to work,' she is reckoning her audience will spot the allusion to the 'weeping prophet' Jeremiah. Or when Michael Foot talks about David Steel as 'the Boy David', he knows his fellow MPs will know he means the David who defeated Goliath.

The danger with allusion is that the reference is so obscure that people don't get it, and the power of the meaning is lost. The point of allusion, like all rhetorical devices, is to enhance the power of words. If a reference to the Bhagavad Gita, an obscure bit of Dryden or a Taylor Swift track fails to land, then it is a waste of words. It might be that the allusion is specific to a particular generation, or a particular sub-stratum of the British class system, or even just whether you watched *Game of Thrones* or not.

John Smith in 1993 assaulted the government by two TV-related allusions:

> If we were to offer that tale of events to the BBC light entertainment department as a script for a programme, I think that the producers of *Yes Minister* would have turned it down as hopelessly over the top. It might have even been too much for *Some Mothers Do 'Ave 'Em*.

Yes, *Yes Minister* is known to every MP, lobby correspondent and most of the people listening to *Today in Parliament*. But *Some Mothers Do 'Ave 'Em* was broadcast between 1973 and 1978 and might be a bit obscure for anyone under forty.

So, if you're going to use a literary allusion:

- Make it relevant to the speech, not a means to try to look clever
- Make it accessible to a broad mass of listeners. Try it out on the young people in your office
- Get it right. As with quotations, there's nothing more likely to set your inbox aflame than a wrongly attributed, muddled-up or inaccurate allusion
- Use allusions that people are likely to 'get'
- Don't try to be trendy or down with the kids, as it won't work

ANECDOTE: THE ONE WHERE YOU TELL A STORY

We all love a good tale. Storytelling is how we make sense of the world, entertain ourselves and each other, build myths and make a point. We use anecdotes in a speech, not just to entertain and change the pace, tone and style of a speech but also to link to the main point of the speech. The story is the carrier of the broader message of the speech.

For example, here is Alex Norris MP, as a shadow minister, in an Opposition Day debate on tackling knife crime:

> Ronan Kanda was sixteen. He went to get a PlayStation controller from his friend and was yards away from home when he was murdered. He was murdered by two teenagers, who used a ninja sword. They had obtained that sword by buying it online, using someone else's ID to collect it. They stabbed him in a case of mistaken identity. This is a heartbreaking, tragic story of a young life lost, with a family trapped in the most extraordinary grief, and we are here today because it is time that Parliament acts to tackle knife crime head-on.

The story – compelling, tragic, concise – links directly to Alex Norris's argument about controlling zombie knives.

Stories can be funny, self-effacing, poignant, revelatory or shocking, like the one above. They allow the speaker to introduce characters, scenes, mini-plots and voices and change the tempo in the middle of a speech. They draw the Chamber in, if done well.

The speeches MPs made as tributes to the late Queen Elizabeth II were filled with anecdotes, each designed to illuminate some aspect of her character, deeds, and life's work.

For example, here's former Prime Minister Boris Johnson:

> I hope the House will not mind if I begin with a personal confession. A few months ago, the BBC came to see me to

> talk about Her Majesty the Queen. We sat down and the cameras started rolling, and they requested that I should talk about her in the past tense. I am afraid that I simply choked up and could not go on. I am really not easily moved to tears, but I was so overcome with sadness that I had to ask them to go away.

Or Iain Duncan Smith MP, former leader of the Conservative Party:

> Of course, we all have anecdotes. When I ceased being leader of the Conservative Party – it happens quite a lot, so I think the Queen was pretty used to it – she kindly asked me to take leave of her officially. I thought that was pretty kind – nobody else wanted me to, so it was decent of her to do that. When I came to the palace, and I was ushered into her small personal sitting room, I was struck by two or three things. One was the two-bar electric fire, which had around it a very strange piece of cardboard in the shape of flames and coloured with yellow and red crayons – I suspect by somebody in the palace. It surrounded the fire, and I thought that was peculiarly dangerous; notwithstanding that, I am sure it had a purpose. The other thing was the Tupperware radio sitting next to her. I had not seen one since my parents smashed their last one. She very sweetly asked me how I was, being clearly sympathetic about what had happened. I just shrugged and said, 'Well, Ma'am, nobody died and I'm

> still here,' whereupon she roared with laughter. The funny thing was that she then paused and looked at me, not sure whether I had actually made a joke. I laughed too, and then she laughed again – whether at me or with me, I could not figure out. That was something to relish.

This contains many of the key elements of a good anecdote. It is personal and revelatory. It is self-effacing and humorous. The use of details such as the two-bar electric fire adds some colour. I'm not sure Iain Duncan Smith meant a 'Tupperware radio', which doesn't exist, but perhaps 'Bakelite radio', which does.

Here's the Democratic Unionist Party MP Ian Paisley with an anecdote about the Queen visiting his constituency in Northern Ireland:

> On her last visit to North Antrim, she visited Bushmills. It looked like a box of Quality Street, with a contingent of the Irish Guards decked out in red tunics and Séamus the dog walking through the village. When the Queen arrived to unveil the statue of the war hero Robert Quigg, she said to me as I welcomed her, 'Is this all yours?' I hesitated and said, 'No, Ma'am, this is yours.' With a twinkle in her eye, she said, 'Quite.' [Laughter.] I will never forget it; it was a lovely moment.

See, a story telling a bigger story.

Leo Amery told an anecdote during the Norway debate that

was plainly made up, but the Chamber suspended its collective disbelief because of the power of the point:

> I remember that many years ago in East Africa a young friend of mine went lion hunting. He secured a sleeping car on the railway and had it detached from the train at a siding near where he expected to find a certain man-eating lion. He went to rest and dream of hunting his lion in the morning. Unfortunately, the lion was out man-hunting that night. He clambered on to the rear of the car, scrabbled open the sliding door, and ate my friend. That is in brief the story of our initiative over Norway.

It is vital that the anecdote cannot be easily disproved and thus the member made to look disingenuous or untrustworthy. On occasion, MPs like to embellish aspects of their past, borrow each other's stories, or even just make stuff up for impact. *Every poet is a thief*, as Bono once sang, although he had stolen the phrase from someone else. However, if the fiction outweighs the fact to the point where the anecdote falls over, you need to take it out of the speech.

Anecdote checklist

- The anecdote is a brilliant way to illustrate your speech
- It brings in characters, dialogue, scenes, a plot and a pay-off
- The anecdote must be linked to the theme or message of the speech

- If it's about the MP, it needs to be anchored in the truth (or at least not be disprovable)
- The middle sections of a speech are a good place to put an anecdote to liven things up and wake up the Chamber

QUOTATION: THE ONE WHERE YOU USE SOMEONE ELSE'S WORDS

You can use quotes in your speech to support your argument. They should be short, relevant and accurate. You can use a variety of sources. It could be a quote from an email from a constituent. It could be a quote from a government document or a speech by another MP. It could be a direct lift from some great work of literature such as Shakespeare, Dickens, Shelley or the Bible.

Unlike academic writing, you don't need to give a chapter-and-verse citation about the source of the quote. You may want to put an exact page number on a policy document to show you've read it and you are being accurate. Or you could just drop it in to add some poetry and lyricism to your speech.

Shakespeare is a good standby for allusion. Here's Kevin Brennan MP responding to Chris Webb MP's Maiden Speech:

> I congratulate my hon. friend the Member for Blackpool South [Chris Webb] on his brilliant Maiden Speech. We learned that his wife is called Portia. That is quite appropriate as we are discussing a Justice Bill, given that Portia gave one of the most famous speeches on justice in *The Merchant of Venice*:
>
> The quality of mercy is not strained;

> It droppeth as the gentle rain from heaven
> Upon the place beneath. It is twice blessed;
> It blesseth him that gives and him that takes.

> I am glad he aptly reminded us of his wife's name during the course of his speech. I congratulate him, and I am sure we will be seeing each other again soon – without being complacent in any way about the electorate.

What is impressive is that Brennan is responding to a speech he has just heard in the Chamber and dropping in the quote from *The Merchant of Venice* from memory. Intriguingly, despite the line about seeing each other again soon, Brennan announced he was not standing again a few days later.

Here's Neil Kinnock giving this tribute to John Smith on the day after he died in 1994:

> I am one of many who will remember John Smith with respect for his tenacity and his brilliance and with the deepest affection for his exuberance and his humanity. He was, in Shelley's words, one of those who

> with resolute will
> Vanquished earth's pride and meanness, burst the chains,
> The icy chains of custom, and have shone
> The day-stars of their age.

Indeed he did.

A massive word of warning in using quotations. So many popular quotes that do the rounds are just plain wrong. Either they are wrongly attributed, or they are things that the famous person never said. For example, loads of MPs quote the founder of the NHS, Aneurin Bevan, as saying, 'The NHS will last as long as there's folk with faith left to fight for it.' Except he didn't. The words come from a 1997 television play about the Welsh politician: *Food for Ravens*, by Trevor Griffiths. That doesn't stop politicians sonorously repeating the words like Holy Writ. The website quoteinvestigator.com is a good starting point to check the veracity of your quote before you say it out loud in the Chamber and risk the tuts and raised eyebrows of your colleagues.

Quotation checklist

- Quoting documents, Hansard, manifestos and so on is a good way to support your argument
- You can quote poets, playwrights, novelists, movies, speeches and journalists
- But GET IT RIGHT

EUPHEMISM: THE ONE WHERE YOU SOFTEN THE BLOW

Euphemism means substituting softer-sounding words or phrases to disguise a difficult or upsetting description. The two areas that leap to mind are death and going to the toilet. When someone dies, we perhaps talk about them passing away, kicking the bucket, pushing up the daisies, cashing in their chips, giving up the ghost or simply falling asleep.

For going to the toilet, we speak of spending a penny, powdering our nose, doing our business, seeing a man about a dog, using the facilities and dozens of cruder versions. We might talk about 'unmentionables' instead of underwear, 'in the family way' instead of pregnant, or 'tired and emotional' or 'three sheets to the wind' to mean drunk.

In July 1983, Clare Short MP, then a newly elected Labour backbencher, believed that the minister speaking at the Despatch Box, Alan Clark, was drunk. He was, as he cheerfully admitted in his *Diaries*.

But Short struggled to find the right euphemism, as the exchange with the Deputy Speaker shows:

> *Ms Short:*
> On a point of order, Mr Deputy Speaker. I have read in the newspapers that in the House one is not allowed to accuse another hon. member of not being sober. However, I seriously put it to you that the minister is incapable. [Hon. members withdraw.] It is disrespectful to the House and to the office that he holds for the hon. gentleman to come here.
>
> *Mr Deputy Speaker*:
> Order. The hon. lady ought not to make allegations of that kind. She should withdraw.
>
> *Ms Short*:
> I shall not withdraw.

Hon. members:
Withdraw.

Mr Deputy Speaker:
Order. The hon. lady should withdraw the allegation.

Hon. members:
Withdraw.

Ms Short:
No. I am speaking the truth.

Mr Deputy Speaker:
Order. The hon. lady should withdraw the allegation.

Mr Michael Brown (Brigg and Cleethorpes):
Name her.

Ms Short:
I should be grateful for your advice, Mr Deputy Speaker. I mean what I say, but I do not understand the rules of the House. How am I allowed to tell the House that I mean it, without being penalised for saying it?

Mr Deputy Speaker:
Order. I understand how the hon. lady feels. She has not been long in the House. However, she really ought to

> withdraw that allegation. It is not permitted to accuse an hon. member in that way.
>
> *Hon. members:*
> Withdraw.

Clark's *Diaries* record the incident in its full horror. He was undoubtedly worse for wear after a wine tasting involving the '61 Palmer, the '75 Palmer for comparison, then more of the '61, then a bottle of Pichon Longueville. There was only one other person present. Arriving at the House, the minister realised that the speech his officials had prepared for him was really bad.

The *Diaries* record:

> Give a civil servant a good case and he'll wreck it with clichés, bad punctuation, double negatives and convoluted apology ... Helter skelter I galloped through the text. Sometimes I turned over two pages at once, sometimes three. What did it matter? There was no shape to it. No linkage from one proposition to another. The very antithesis of an Aristotelian pattern.

The minister can always blame the officials for a poor speech, but I doubt the four bottles of wine helped, as Clare Short was rightly pointing out.

Perhaps the most famous euphemism in Parliament is 'terminological inexactitude', meaning a lie, which was coined by Winston Churchill, then Under-Secretary of the Colonial Office, in February 1906. When asked if the government was using Chinese slaves in South Africa, he replied:

'The conditions of the Transvaal ordinance ... cannot in the opinion of His Majesty's government be classified as slavery; at least, that word in its full sense could not be applied without a risk of terminological inexactitude.'

This has since become a knowing way for parliamentarians to call each other liars without using the (unparliamentary) word.

Here's Margaret Thatcher in the no-confidence debate on 28 March 1979:

'From his days as Home Secretary we know that the right hon. gentleman takes what might be charitably described as a flexible view of constitutional niceties...'

In that same debate, Michael Foot said of Thatcher they had 'exchanged occasional pleasantries' as a euphemism for their great ideological clashes.

You use euphemism when you want to avoid offence, or to lessen the power of your words, or to be humorous.

Euphemism checklist

- Parliamentary style is to avoid direct references to taboo subjects such as death, sex, drunkenness and so on
- Euphemism allows you to soften the blow

IMAGERY: THE ONE WHERE YOU PAINT PICTURES

Because speeches are a sound-based medium, with the impact

designed for the ear not the eye, imagery is an effective device to deploy. You paint pictures with words – using colours, sizes, shapes or images that are already in people's memory banks. The trick is to paint pictures that your audience can easily conjure up. You can see in your mind's eye a big blue bear, but you can't see the hydron collider.

Here's Rosena Allin-Khan MP paying tribute to the late Queen:

> Some recall her service in the British Army when, with invasion imminent, she could have fled to Canada; instead, she stayed in London and put on a khaki uniform and a tin helmet. I remember best her service during the pandemic. Suffering the grief of the loss of her dear husband Philip, she cut a lonely figure at his funeral as she observed social distancing. She embodied the pain that so many people were experiencing at the same time and she led, truly, by example. She was a shining beacon of light in that dark moment and never once deviated from her duty.

I like the use of 'khaki uniform and a tin helmet', which paints a familiar picture of army uniform, and 'lonely figure', which summons up the image of the Queen alone during the pandemic.

In May 2024, Andrew Gwynne MP quizzed the Foreign Office Minister on the disaster unfolding in Sudan:

> I intend no disrespect to the minister, but the government's

> response just does not seem to be as robust as it could be given the severity of the situation in Sudan, which is horrific. She will have read reports in *The Guardian* about children – alive children – being 'piled up and shot' by RSF paramilitaries in El Geneina. What mechanisms are the government considering to prevent this genocide from spreading to El Fasher?

The statistics are horrific, but the imagery makes the point even more forcibly.

Imagery checklist

- Paint pictures with your words. A picture is worth a thousand words
- Use colours, shapes, sizes and textures
- Use comparisons – the size of a football field etc.
- An image is more powerful than a number

REPETITION: THE ONE WHERE YOU SAY THE SAME THING MORE THAN ONCE, MORE THAN ONCE

Speechwriting is one of those artforms that uses repetition as a deliberate method of reinforcement, emphasis, to generate anticipation and to give rhythm. Like the refrain in a poem, or the chorus in a song, or the leitmotif in a symphony, we use repetition of key words or phrases in speeches. If you did it in an article or briefing, you would strike it out. If you did it in casual conversation, the other person's eyes would glass over. But in a speech, it can be majestic.

There are two kinds of repetition. One is to repeat the key phrase at the start of the sentence or clause (*anaphora*) and the other is to repeat at the end (*epistrophe*). For *anaphora*, think Churchill's 'we shall fight on the beaches', delivered to the House of Commons in June 1940. This is the famous peroration:

> Even though large tracts of Europe and many old and famous States have fallen or may fall into the grip of the Gestapo and all the odious apparatus of Nazi rule, we shall not flag or fail. We shall go on to the end. We shall fight in France, we shall fight on the seas and oceans, we shall fight with growing confidence and growing strength in the air, we shall defend our island, whatever the cost may be. We shall fight on the beaches, we shall fight on the landing grounds, we shall fight in the fields and in the streets, we shall fight in the hills; we shall never surrender. And even if, which I do not for a moment believe, this island or a large part of it were subjugated and starving, then our Empire beyond the seas, armed and guarded by the British Fleet, would carry on the struggle, until, in God's good time, the New World, with all its power and might, steps forth to the rescue and the liberation of the Old.

You can hear how 'we shall fight' is repeated at the start of each clause, half a dozen times. There's more to this than merely a rhetorical flourish. Churchill was trying to shore up support for his policy of fighting a war against Germany, when many of his own party, and beyond, wanted to avoid one at all costs. Churchill uses *anaphora* to reinforce the key part of the argument he is writing to win. It's not accidental.

In the peroration of 'I Have a Dream', Martin Luther King Jr says, 'With this faith we will be able to work together, to pray together, to struggle together, to go to jail together, to stand up for freedom together, knowing that we will be free one day.' The *epistrophe* on the word 'together' is no accident either. King is trying to win an argument about the unity of the civil rights movement in the face of Black Nationalists who wanted a more separatist approach. The lesson is that if you have something important to say, say it more than once.

Repetition checklist

- Repetition is an important rhetorical device for emphasis and reinforcement
- Use it at the start or the end, or mix it up
- Repeat the important message, not just random phrases

METAPHOR: THE ONE WHERE YOU SAY SOMETHING IS SOMETHING ELSE

A metaphor is a rhetorical device or figure of speech that says a thing is another thing, to make a point, capture the imagination or illuminate the argument.

It can be a simple metaphor such as the 'Red Wall' – the description loosely used to describe hitherto Labour-held parliamentary seats, often with long traditions within the Labour and trade union movement, which fell to the Conservatives in

2019. See also 'Blue Wall', 'Grey Wall', or 'Sea Wall' to describe different types of seat and demographics.

Or as straightforward as Chancellor Rachel Reeves in July 2024 stating her desire to 'fix the foundations of our economy'.

Or Michael Ancram MP during the Iraq debate in 2003, speaking of Saddam Hussein: 'Instead, he has chosen to take the international community to the wire.'

The wire is the final stage of a race.

Or Tony Wright MP during the same debate: 'We knew that Saddam Hussein could be disarmed only through a process that was like drawing teeth.'

This metaphor drew the attention of the Foreign Secretary Jack Straw MP, who picked up the baton:

> Drawing teeth is not just difficult but is possible only if the patient has his mouth open. In the case of Saddam Hussein, if I may continue the analogy, we have a patient who most of the time has his mouth closed and who from time to time bites the dentist. In those circumstances, achieving compliance from this so-called patient to draw the teeth becomes impossible.

Reform MP Richard Tice suggested that removing a drugs dealer from the street corner is 'like a game of whack-a-mole: another one will appear and then another one'.

Here's Lloyd George to Churchill during the Norway debate in 1940:

'The right honourable gentleman must not allow himself to

be converted into an air-raid shelter to keep the splinters from hitting his colleagues.'

Why does it work? Because it's humorous, and yet the choice of metaphor fits into the zeitgeist of a nation preparing for air raids. Roy Jenkins, in his book about Churchill, described the metaphor as 'brilliant'.

Or you could use an 'extended metaphor', which runs the device over several sentences. Here's Geoffrey Howe's famous resignation speech in 1990, when he puts the boot into Margaret Thatcher in seemingly urbane but deadly style:

> I believe that both the Chancellor and the Governor are cricketing enthusiasts, so I hope that there is no monopoly of cricketing metaphors. It is rather like sending your opening batsmen to the crease only for them to find, the moment the first balls are bowled, that their bats have been broken before the game by the team captain.

George Orwell in *Politics and the English Language* points to the dangers of metaphors-gone-wrong. A 'dead' metaphor is one where the words have reverted to being ordinary and have therefore lost all vividness and impact, for example, 'kick the bucket'. Worn-out metaphors that Orwell lists include 'ring the changes on', 'toe the line', 'ride roughshod over', 'stand shoulder to shoulder with', 'Achilles' heel' and 'hotbed'. These, he says, are merely used to save people the trouble of inventing phrases for themselves (which we will take from the man who coined 'cold war', 'unperson', 'doublethink', 'Big Brother' and 'Room 101').

Modern politics is littered with examples of metaphors that have become so commonplace they fall into cliché. Browse Hansard and you are likely to rub up against 'blank cheque', 'can of worms', 'political football', 'bloodstream', 'sunset clause', 'landslide victory', 'paper candidate', 'grassroots', 'sacred cow', 'straw man', 'lame duck', 'witch-hunt', 'stalking horse' or 'reverse ferret'. They are lazy and lack impact because they are unoriginal.

In his noted speech on Syria in December 2015, Hilary Benn MP uses the following metaphor: 'What should we do with others to confront this threat to our citizens, our nation, other nations and the people who suffer under the yoke, the cruel yoke, of Daesh?'

What's a cruel yoke? Some might think it refers to the yellow bit of eggs. A few might understand a 'yoke' relates to the heavy wooden device to harness cattle or oxen.

Does it matter if people don't get the reference? Some theorists, for example George Lakoff and Mark Johnson in their *Metaphors We Live By* (1980) argue there is no such thing as a dead metaphor because the phrase has become part of our shared language and culture and takes on meaning of its own, regardless of whether we appreciate its origins.

For example, in British English in particular, there are dozens of phrases that belie Britain's history as a naval power, which we use without necessarily knowing their meaning, like 'show a leg', 'let the cat out of the bag', 'pipe down', 'pull your finger out', 'over a barrel', 'long shot', 'at loggerheads', 'true colours', 'above board', 'piping hot', 'square meal', 'feeling groggy', 'batten down the hatches' and 'freeze the balls off a brass monkey'. Each of these might be used in a speech in the right context, without the audience needing to understand their nautical roots.

Worse, perhaps, than a dead or dying metaphor is a mangled or mixed metaphor. For example Ernie Bevin's view on the idea of a Council of Europe in 1948: 'I don't like it. When you open that Pandora's box, you will find it full of Trojan horses.'

Or this exchange in *Yes Minister*:

> Sir Desmond: If you spill the beans, you open up a whole can of worms. How can you let sleeping dogs lie if you let the cat out of the bag? Bring in a new broom, and if you're not careful, you'll find you've thrown the baby out with the bath water. If you change horses in the middle of the stream, next thing you know you're up the creek without a paddle.
>
> Jim Hacker: And then the balloon goes up.
>
> Sir Desmond: Obviously.

This is a well-trodden path, but you must be careful with the word 'literally'. Literally means the thing actually happened, is real, existing, tangible or concrete. It does not mean metaphorically. So when the much-loved and much-missed Tessa Jowell MP told the House, 'It provides an opportunity to deal with what are literally shoals of red herrings swirling around the issue…' she did not mean there were actually shoals of red herrings.

Do not confuse metaphor with simile, which is a slightly different kettle of fish. A simile is when you say something is as … as something else. For example, if a particular MP was referred to as being 'thick as mince', that's a simile.

Metaphor checklist

- Metaphors can make sense of what you're describing
- Choose simple, easy-to-see metaphors
- Don't mix metaphors
- Avoid dead metaphors
- Keep it fresh and avoid clichés

HUMOUR: THE ONE WHERE YOU'RE FUNNY

It is obvious that what passes for humour in the House of Commons would not pass muster on *Live at the Apollo*. The bar for parliamentary humour is set so low you can hardly see daylight. As Ed Balls admits, 'Whisper it quietly, but almost none of the jokes we tell are actually, well, funny.' On the other hand, humour can be used waspishly, cunningly and intelligently to undermine an opponent's argument, derail a minister or gain favour in the Chamber.

Baroness Hazarika, better known as Ayesha, is a new Labour member of the House of Lords and has honed her oratorical skills as a pundit, presenter, politician, panellist and an actual stand-up comic. Her Maiden Speech in the Lords was a well-crafted affair and, as you might have hoped, had a couple of good jokes:

> I grew up in Coatbridge in the county of Lanarkshire, near Glasgow. My father was the local GP there for many, many years. It was tough for my parents when they first arrived from a different country. People were very curious. One of my dad's patients said to him, 'What are you?' 'A Muslim,' he replied. 'Aye, but what kind? A Rangers Muslim or a Celtic Muslim?'

I am absolutely sure that this happened exactly as described, but luckily it also echoes the old joke about a Jewish man walking into a pub in the Falls Road. The next joke is also quality:

> My mum and dad came from Assam in India, where the tea comes from. Many of you will have enjoyed a cup of Assam tea. It is an area to the north of the country where it rains a lot and they are fighting for independence. My parents fancied a real change of scene so they moved to Scotland, an area where – you get the picture.

The punchline is in the minds of the listener. They anticipate it and say it in their own heads before the speaker has to. The line, then, is unsaid. We are all in on the joke.

Next, this joke plays on the Indian parent stereotype and their ambition for their sons and daughters to become lawyers or doctors. Note how Baroness Hazarika shifts gear from the heartfelt and heartwarming story of her parents arriving from Assam to Coatbridge with £3 in their pocket to the punchline.

> I am so glad that my parents chose to settle in Coatbridge. They say that to be Scottish is a gift and I very much believe that to be true. I feel truly humbled by my parents' courage. Theirs is the classic story of the immigrant. They came here in the 1960s to work and build up the NHS, with £3 in their pocket, in a cold climate, yet they built such a good and happy life here for me and my brother. I pay tribute to them as first-generation immigrants for their work ethic, decency, good humour and desire to make friends with people from all different backgrounds – qualities that I hope to replicate in this House. On the big day, my father's former receptionist, Monica, messaged me to say, 'Ayesha, they are so very proud of you, but they do still wish you had become a doctor.'

Humour is often about subversion of what is expected, a sudden change of mood, a surprise, or a shock. Sigmund Freud suggested that jokes are a steam valve for forbidden thoughts suppressed deep in our psyche, which explains the success of Ricky Gervais.

It's about misdirection, then a reveal at the end. The first part of a joke is based on playing on shared audience assumptions and then slamming on the handbrake. So with Ayesha's joke, we might have assumed the message from Monica to say how proud the parents are that their daughter made it into the House of Lords. To hear they wish she had become a doctor is not what we expected, and so it's funny.

In his tribute to Baroness Hazarika's Maiden Speech, Lord Davies of Oldham said:

> I suspect that most noble Lords will be keen to talk to my noble friend about her appearances on *Have I Got News for You*. She has demonstrated that she will be a popular speaker. People may well come for the jokes, but they will stay for the serious political points being made.

These are wise words, because in Parliament humour must be used for some motive purpose, not merely for entertainment.

The truth is that writing comedy is a hugely complex and difficult task. During lockdown, I did a comedy writing course online, and it revealed to me that I am not very good at it. Speechwriters are sometimes asked for 'a couple of jokes', as though we have a cupboard full of them, but humour is a tricky alchemy of speaker, audience, context and delivery. If you can write jokes, ones that people really laugh at, move to Hollywood. It's a rare and wonderful gift. Don't waste it on Parliament.

There are some genuinely funny MPs. William Hague has a brilliant combination of wit, pinpoint timing and northern working men's club accent. I've seen Hague's after-dinner act and he deserves every penny of his substantial speaking fees. Stephen Pound is probably the funniest person in the Labour Party. Tony Banks was a master of mockery. Dennis Skinner was famous for his acerbic noises-off during the State Opening of Parliament. Gordon Brown had a stock of jokes that were taken out time and time again like fine china. He had the perspicacity to hire a couple of actual comedy writers, John O'Farrell and John Langdon, to write jokes.

In 1991, Dennis Healey MP welcomed the new Conservative Prime Minister John Major. Healey was capable of great humour. Here he uses an allusion to *Peanuts* to make a joke at the new PM's expense.

> All of us like the Prime Minister and it is difficult to be rude about him – I have not yet attempted it – but I must confess that he reminds me of one of the most notable characters in current folklore – Charlie Brown in *Peanuts*. You may remember, Mr Speaker, because I am sure that you are an avid follower of *Peanuts*, that Charlie Brown was once approached by Lucy – a bossy little girl – [Laughter.] The parallel escapes me. Lucy asked Charlie to join her on an ocean cruise, so they got on the boat and she took Charlie up to the sun deck and said to Charlie, 'Now, Charlie, there you will see a stack of deckchairs, and you have to put your deckchair up – and Charlie, if you want to look backwards, you put it facing the stern of the boat' – which she obviously preferred herself – 'but if you want to look forward into the future, you place it facing the prow of the boat.' 'Now, Charlie,' she said, 'which way do you want your deckchair facing? Charlie replied – so much like the Prime Minister – 'I don't seem able to get my deckchair unfolded.'

> I hope, without great confidence, that the Prime Minister will manage to get his deckchair unfolded at some time in the next twelve months. But, of course, after twelve months, the liner will be under a different captain.

Ed Balls writes, 'Done well, humour, self-deprecation or mockery of your opponents can get an audience going, establish a connection, or – in Parliament – ram home a point. But the actual process of coming up with jokes, lines and anecdotes is extremely tortured, time-consuming and stressful – and certainly no laughing matter.'

The best kind of humour is not cruel jibes aimed at your opponents but instead humour directed at yourself. This is self-effacing humour, showing strength of character and self-confidence.

In July 2024, Georgia Gould MP recalled that after she was elected to Camden Council in 2010,

> people used to say to me, 'What do you do?' I would proudly say to them, 'I am a councillor.' They would say, 'That is so wonderful, you do such wonderful work as a therapist.' I would have to say, 'No, not that kind of counsellor, I am a Labour Party councillor…'

Or here's Luke Akehurst MP: 'It has taken me some time to get elected to the House. I first stood in a general election back in 2001, so no one can accuse me of being a young man in a rush.' These kinds of humorous references to the self are the product of confident politicians who are comfortable in their own skins. You cannot imagine Donald Trump making a self-effacing joke.

If you are seeking to use humour in your parliamentary speeches, here are some tips:

- Is it funny? The acid test is to try it out on some of your friends. If the MP thinks it's hilarious and you don't, here's the best moment to speak truth to power
- Is it offensive? Honestly, it is possible to be funny without offending anyone, so try it. And if you do want to offend someone, punch upwards not downwards. It's okay to offend Vladimir Putin
- Is it short? A short humorous line can be swiftly moved on from if it fails to land, but a long joke building to a punchline, if followed by tumbleweed, is impossible to recover from

CHAPTER FIVE

A WORD OR TWO ON DELIVERY

It is a little-known fact that the Chamber of the House of Commons is a big fat fake. How old do you think it is? As old as Westminster Hall, dating from the reign of Rufus? Or only as old as the Elizabeth Tower housing Big Ben, which is mid-Victorian? In fact, the Chamber of the House of Commons is only as old as the National Theatre on the South Bank, with all of its concrete and steel modernism, and younger than one or two Members of the House of Lords.

The original Chamber was extensively remodelled in 1941 by the Germans, when the Luftwaffe dropped incendiary bombs and burnt the place to sticks. This was all hushed up during the war, lest it damaged morale, although the previous time the place burned down, Londoners took to the streets and cheered each falling rafter. Churchill insisted that the rebuilt Chamber should take on the appearance of the previous one, so the chance for an open, horseshoe-shaped Chamber with seats for everyone and perhaps even electronic voting, was missed. Instead, the Chamber is crowded and noisy, because Churchill wanted the intimacy and drama.

He told Parliament, meeting down at the House of Lords end of the building, 'We shape our buildings; thereafter they shape us,' on 28 October 1943 as he argued that the House of Commons be rebuilt from the rubble and embers exactly as before. He wanted a 'cockpit of the nation'. That's why we have the cacophonous, gladiatorial Chamber that the public love so much. This, of course, affects the way speeches are delivered and how they must be written. The Chamber is not a place which rewards subtlety or nuance. A quiet voice is easily ignored or drowned out. The Chamber can sense fear, like dogs.

Demosthenes, the Athenian orator and speechwriter, is reputed to have said that the three most important elements of a speech were 'delivery, delivery, delivery'. It is certainly true that the content of your speech is only as good as the way it is delivered. Or is it? In Parliament, few people are listening in the Chamber, and not many more are listening outside. The way people will receive your brilliant arguments may well be via Hansard, after you've emailed it to them, or just a short clip on social media. What looks good on the page may have sounded terrible in the Chamber.

Notwithstanding the absence of a mass audience, there should be some attention given to the delivery of a speech. The writer can help here, with short sentences, easy-to-pronounce words and a clear structure with signposts.

I wrote a speech for the shadow rail minister about electrification of the railway in South Wales, which involved Welsh place names. Many of these are hard for English people to pronounce, so the advice here is to spell tricky words out phonetically. Don't suddenly come across Troed-y-rhiw, Ystrad Mynach, or Rhiwbina in a speech without a clear idea of how to say them out loud.

You're not really allowed to read out a script, as we have seen. On occasion, MPs get called out for it. Here's Angela Rayner, the Deputy Prime Minister, being challenged by Andrew Griffith:

> *Andrew Griffith:*
> You are just reading! You are supposed to be answering the questions, not just reading out what has been written for you to read.
>
> *Angela Rayner:*
> These are the answers to the questions.
> [*Interruption.*]
> No, they are the bits that I have written, actually, in regard to her questions.

You can use the A5 parliamentary notepaper, cue cards or a tablet, but far more impressive is to remember what you want to say and speak without notes. My advice to speakers is to have some notes nearby just in case, as you may be overwhelmed by the moment and your mind may go blank.

A word to the wise: make sure that any stage directions are firmly distinct from the text and do not read them out. A minister in the House of Lords is supposed to have declared in a debate:

'This is a rotten argument, but it is good enough for their Lordships on a hot summer afternoon.'

Speakers in the Chamber stand to speak, if they are able to. The rules state that 'you should face the Chair when addressing the House. It is discourteous to turn your back on the Chair. It also means that your words may be lost.'

Breathe deeply and speak slowly. Like an actor, build in some pauses to look across the Chamber and make eye contact. You can even stop and hold a few seconds of silence for dramatic impact. As any stand-up or actor will tell you, it's all about the space between sounds. Ralph Richardson, the great thespian, said, 'The most precious things in a speech are pauses. A pause will fill the void, capture attention; it will punctuate, illuminate and build the tension in a speech.' Don't forget the old truth that a pause will seem like an echoing eternity to the speaker but a welcome chance to catch up for the audience.

The Chamber has microphones dangling from the ceiling and cameras strategically placed around the walls, so MPs need to face forward and speak clearly. Try to avoid being obscured on the TV shots by the dangling microphones. The first televised speech was in November 1989 by Eastbourne MP Ian Gow, where he recounted receiving a letter from 'image consultants' sent to all MPs:

> I have always voted against the televising of the proceedings of this House, and I expect that I always will. The brief intervention earlier of the hon. gentleman the Member for

> Bradford, South [Mr Cryer] did nothing to alter my view. Despite the strongly held opinions which I have on these matters, I received a letter – three weeks ago – I believe that a copy was sent to each of us and possibly even to you, Mr Speaker – which made the following preposterous assertion, and I quote: 'The impression you make on television depends mainly on your image (55 per cent) with your voice and body language accounting for 38 per cent of your impact. Only 7 per cent depends on what you are actually saying.' [Hon. members: 'Hear, hear.'] I thought that I should enlist the sympathy of the opposition with that last proposition. The letter went on – and you may think that this is an extravagant claim so far as I myself am concerned – 'We can guarantee to improve your appearance through a personal and confidential image consultation. You will learn if you need a new hair style – and where to get it – and the type of glasses to suit your face.' The House will understand why I considered that I was beyond redemption on both counts.

On a sombre tangent, I found myself on a long walk in East Sussex that took me to Hankham, and the spot where Ian Gow was assassinated by the IRA in 1990. The IRA bombers looked up his address in *Who's Who* and placed 2kg of Semtex under his Austin Montego. Standing by the driveway twenty-four years later, I reminded myself that parliamentary democracy comes at a price.

The letter sent to MPs repeats the oft-misused study by Albert Mehrabian that suggests that words only matter for '7 per cent' of the speech, with 93 per cent being tone of voice and non-verbal communication. This is of course utter garbage. The study rests on the communication of emotions, where sad news communicated with a grin, or happy news communicated with a frown, is subverted by the facial expression. Of course words matter.

USE OF PROPS

You're not allowed to use props in the Chamber, including maps, charts, newspapers or magazines. You can wave your order paper. One or two members have flouted the rules. John McDonnell, as shadow Chancellor, used a copy of Chairman Mao's 'Little Red Book' to try to get one over on Chancellor George Osborne. Osborne responded with, 'Oh look! It's his personal signed copy,' which was not what McDonnell had hoped. Another Corbynite MP, Zarah Sultana, waved her student loan statement under the nose of the Education Secretary. In general, avoid props.

WHAT TO WEAR?

There are MPs who dress to impress, with flamboyant clothing choices to grab attention. Augustus Henry Fitzroy was Prime Minister from 1768 to 1770 and denounced as a 'macaroni' or dandy for his outlandish dress. Anthony Eden rocked the homburg hat and lounge suit look in the Chamber, and those looking closely detected his use of nail varnish. Disraeli was a proper fashionista, with bold colours like scarlet, purple and gold, and eye-catching accessories like white gloves.

Churchill, of course, had more costume changes than Elton John. Margaret Thatcher wore hats. Keir Hardie caused quite a stir by turning up to Parliament in a tweed suit, red tie and deerstalker hat, at a time when MPs wore frock coats, silk top hats and starched collars. Down the decades, the serried ranks of MPs in sombre suits have been punctuated by peacocks.

The official guidance is that 'the way in which you dress should demonstrate respect for your constituents, for the House and for the institution of Parliament in the life of the nation. Members are expected to wear business attire in and around the Chamber.' I interpret that as meaning dress like it's a job interview.

That means no jeans, chinos, sportswear or any other casual trousers. Men are encouraged to wear a tie, although this rule was relaxed in the hot summer of 2017 by Speaker Bercow. Speaker Hoyle has changed 'encouraged' to 'expected' to wear a tie, so we may see more men in ties in future parliaments, not fewer.

You must wear a jacket, but not scarves, T-shirts, badges or medals, if you have them. In 2013, Harriet Harman tried her luck with a 'This is what a feminist looks like' T-shirt. The Green MP Caroline Lucas was told off by the chair of a Westminster Hall debate for wearing a 'No More Page Three' T-shirt.

Most weeks, there's a commemorative ribbon of some kind. It might be a daffodil for St David's Day, or a red ribbon on World Aids Day, or a Royal British Legion poppy in early November. You can pick these up, depending on your preferences, around the House, and from the party offices within the estate. MPs don't want to get caught out not wearing the appropriate symbol, especially on the front bench.

Your speech will hopefully be worthy of amplification across your social media channels, so you need to consider how your sartorial choices will look on camera. You may even get on the TV. So choose wisely. You can go for plain, unadorned and business-like. You can go for drama and colour. But make sure everything is functioning, no zip is unzipped, nothing is on show that you don't intend, and there's no spinach or lipstick on your teeth.

ACCENTS

The House of Commons reflects the rich and varied accents of the peoples of these islands. You can hear the accents of every part of the United Kingdom and every corner of the country, from Birmingham to Belfast. This is a good thing. The days are gone when most MPs spoke with home counties accents, honed in the Oxford Union and untroubled by the influence of whichever seat sent them to Parliament. Those with 'an accent' (and everyone has an accent) would even attempt to alter it to fit in.

MPs should remain true to their own accents and never try to mask the authenticity of where they are from and how they speak there. If MPs try to sound like the BBC announcers of old, it sounds phony and false.

There may even be the opportunity for dialect words to slip in. For example, Mrs Thatcher had a go at Denis Healey in

1983 in the lead-up to the election: 'The right hon. gentleman is afraid of an election, is he? Afraid? Frightened? Frit? Could not take it? Cannot stand it?'

The word 'frit' is a dialect word for 'scared' or 'frightened' and must have come to Thatcher from the depths of her memories of childhood in Grantham, as she searched for synonyms to hammer home her point. A few dialect words, as long as they are authentically yours, can add some richness and interest to a speech and make it stand out.

Delivery checklist

- People are watching. Attend to your appearance and movement during a speech
- Abide by the sartorial rules. No trainers, no tracksuits, no slogan T-shirts
- Speak facing forward so the microphones can pick up what you're saying (and Hansard can transcribe your words)
- Don't sway or rock, bob or stagger. Just anchor your feet, stand up straight, and don't wave your arms around
- Remember to breathe slowly and deeply

CONCLUSION

MAKING THE WEATHER

George Orwell wrote in *Politics and the English Language* that

> when one watches some tired hack on the platform mechanically repeating the familiar phrases – bestial atrocities, iron heel, blood-stained tyranny, free people of the world, stand shoulder to shoulder – one often has a curious feeling that one is not watching a live human being but some kind of dummy … A speaker who uses that kind of phraseology has gone some distance towards turning himself into a machine.

Alas, many speeches in Parliament are mechanistic. Clunky language. Clichés and jargon. Lifeless prose. As passionate as a squashed slug. Yet sometimes, the machine comes to life.

Consider the appearance of Craig Mackinlay MP in the House of Commons in May 2024, after losing all his limbs to sepsis. His is a remarkable story of resilience and fortitude, and his presence in the Chamber was the cause for admiration across the House. I found watching this speech profoundly moving.

> Thank you, Mr Speaker. This is an emotional day for me, and if you will indulge me, I will say a few thanks, because a few are due. Apologies are due, actually, as I have caused the breaking of so many rules today: there has been clapping; I have got trainers on because my shoes would not go over the plastic feet; and my jacket would not go over the bionic arm.
>
> First, I thank you, Mr Speaker, for being there for me and for coming to visit. I will tell everybody this little story: the rest of the hospital thought I must be dreadfully ill, because they said, 'That guy's got the funeral director in already.' [Laughter.] But you have been, and you have cared for me throughout, and I thank you for that. The other person in this Chamber I would like to thank is the Prime Minister, who has been with me throughout. He has not advertised it, but he has been to see me multiple times. To me, that shows the true depth of the character of the Prime Minister, and I thank him for that.
>
> I thank my wife, who is in the Chamber, my daughter and other family members – my father and my father-in-law. I thank my wife for being there every single day of those many months in hospital. She could only do that because of the support of family behind her. In the public gallery – they cannot quite see me, unfortunately – are many of the staff from the NHS. [Applause.] They took me from where

I was, close to death, to where I am today, so I thank them for that. I am not entirely sure I am that happy that the two surgeons who took this lot off are there, but never mind.

There is a question here. Prime Minister, can we please ensure that we embed recognition of early signs of sepsis? It would not have worked for me – mine was too quick and too sudden – but many people do get a few days. If we can stop somebody from ending up like this, I would say that that is a job well done. I would also like to impress upon Health Ministers the importance of allowing the provision of appropriate prosthetics, particularly for multi-limb amputees, at the right time. Thank you, Mr Speaker; thank you, Prime Minister. [Applause.]

This is an example of a speech that makes the weather. It will undoubtedly help in the fight to raise awareness about sepsis and why we need a cure. Parliament at its best can meet the challenges of the age and deliver a better life for the citizen.

It is important not to fall into lazy nostalgia for a golden past age. The historian Simon Schama, in 2007, lamented that 'by and large the digital age is cool to rhetoric and, as the enthronement of the blogger suggests, prizes incoherent impulse over the Ciceronian arts of the *exordium* and the peroration'.

The reason why F. E. Smith, Lloyd George, Winston Churchill and Barbara Castle are famous for their speeches is because they were the exceptions to the rule, not exemplars of a historically more superior class of politician. We have a far better class of parliamentarian today. And it is always worth remembering that great orators are made, not born. Churchill taught himself how to speak in public; he was no natural. He learned the speeches of Disraeli, Gladstone, Pitt, Burke and Cromwell off by heart and recited them out loud to learn about language, rhythm and pace. Amid the Churchills who learned and mastered their craft, there were multitudes of MPs who didn't bother.

In W. Ivor Jennings's *Parliament* (published in 1939), the author describes how MPs conducted themselves well into the twentieth century:

> Certainly the House of Commons is not composed either wholly or in substantial part of professional politicians. Most members have businesses or professions to conduct. They can, therefore, attend to their own affairs in the day and the nation's in the evening. Indeed, provided that a quorum is left in the House and a majority on the government side, they can also attend to their pleasure in the evening and obey the whip near 10 o'clock at night ... Tea, dinner and a theatre may thus be enjoyed in the interval, and taxis disgorge their loads at 9.45 p.m. to vote for or against the government.

This is the 1930s, not the 1830s. MPs as chaps with day jobs in the City or at the Bar, popping in to Parliament to vote after a night at the theatre.

Denis Healey, in his *The Time of My Life*, recalls that even after the Labour landslide in 1945

> the House of Commons was still run on the assumption that politics was something which wealthy gentlemen did in their spare time. Parliament was simply the best club in London. There were some MPs who never spoke in the chamber and had never asked a question, turning up only to vote on three-line whips, if then. It was said that one or two never visited their constituencies between general elections.

We have come, thank heavens, a long way.

If you look at footage of the House of Commons even up to 1997, it is a drab, grey affair. There is a huge preponderance of white men in grey suits in their forties and fifties. Combovers and dandruff proliferate. If you look at the speeches by the men in grey suits, they sway, they stagger, they mumble and stumble over their words.

Parliament today is infinitely better than it was thirty years ago, when I first worked there. Better because of its vibrancy and diversity and because MPs are more empathetic, media-savvy and better dressed.

The quality of MPs elected in 2024 raises the bar even further. This is an unfashionable view, but the majority of MPs are there to serve their constituencies and advance the public interest. For every bad apple, there is a barrel-load of decent folk who work incredibly hard, are intelligent and diligent, care deeply about their constituencies and want to spend their time in Parliament doing some good. This is demonstrably preferable to previous parliaments dominated by sycophants, dilettantes, placemen and part-timers. It is not that long since MPs didn't live in their constituencies, treated the Palace of Westminster as the 'best club in London' and popped in from time to time to make a middling-to-terrible speech. For every Churchill, there were a hundred mediocrities.

Don't buy the myth of a past golden age. This is it.

GLOSSARY OF TERMS

Adjournment debate: a short debate at the end of the day, when MPs can raise an issue and the minister must respond. A good speechwriting opportunity.

Alliteration: a rhetorical device where words start with the same sound. '*Strong and stable*,' for example.

Anadiplosis: when you repeat the last word or phrase in a sentence at the start of the next one. For example, Yoda in *Star Wars: Episode I – The Phantom Menace*: 'Fear leads to anger, anger leads to hate, hate leads to… suffering.'

Anaphora: repetition of a word or phrase at the start of a string of sentences to create rhythm and anticipation. Churchill's '*We shall fight…*' is a good example.

Assonance: using words in a speech with similar-sounding syllables. For example, '*I wandered lonely as a cloud / that floats on high o'er vales and hills*'.

Chamber: the space where parliamentary speeches are delivered – one in the Commons and one in the Lords. Because the Commons is crowded and small, it lends itself to gladiatorial and bombastic speechmaking. The Lords' Chamber, by contrast, is more open, less confrontational and supports more thoughtful and deliberative speeches.

Chiasmus: when the writer echoes, or mirrors, the first half of the phrase in the second.

Decorum: the correct and fitting form and tone of a speech for the occasion. Each parliamentary speech has its own decorum.

Despatch Box: these are wooden and brass boxes that front-bench speakers can use to anchor their hands and place their notes. Please never write 'dispatch'. Also the name of the coffee bar in Portcullis House.

Ethos: this is the standing, credibility and reputation of the MP speaking. If the MP has a particular insight into the subject of the speech (a former soldier speaking on the Ukraine war, for example), it is a good idea to establish it early on.

Erskine May: a man and the multi-volume set of rules he wrote.

Exordium: setting out the purpose of the speech and the main thrust of the argument. You set up the promise of what is to come, to create expectation and anticipation.

First Reading: the bill is introduced, but no speeches are made.

Hansard: the official record of everything said in each Chamber plus Westminster Hall, named after Thomas Curson Hansard (1776–1833), a London printer and publisher. Hansard is the go-to resource for speechwriters to see what others have said on the topic.

Hypophora: asking a question in a speech then answering it.

Interventions: in most, but not all, speeches, MPs can interrupt each other to make a point. These can be drafted in advance, using the rhetorical devices of a larger speech. It is up to the MP speaking to decide whether to allow the intervention.

Kairos: roughly translated from the Greek as 'the moment' or the most propitious time for an MP to be speaking.

Logos: the facts, stats, numbers and stone-cold logic of the argument.

King's Speech: when the King reads out all the things 'his' government plans to do in legislation. Also a film about a monarch struggling to make speeches and overcoming his stammer.

Library: the House of Commons one supplies the raw material for every kind of speech. Make friends with everyone who works there.

Maiden Speech: the first formal speech by an MP or peer.

Metaphor: a form of words whereby something is likened to, or simply described as something else. The Houses of Parliament as 'the gasworks', for example. Or Nigel Lawson's description of the Labour Party as 'a squid lost in its own ink'.

Narratio: The middle section of the speech, the building blocks of the argument.

Order Paper: I was taught from an early age to 'always start the day with the Order Paper' before even a cappuccino from the Despatch. This is the A4 document telling you what's happening that day.

Other Place: the colloquial way to describe the House of Lords in a speech (not compulsory but welcomed).

Pathos: appeals in a speech to emotions – love, hate, fear, hope.

Petitions: MPs can present a paper petition on behalf of their bosses, and get about a minute to articulate their concerns.

Points of Order: an MP asks the Speaker for guidance on a point of procedure, or more usually makes a mini political speech before being closed down.

Portcullis House: the building next to the 'main building' of Parliament, sitting over Westminster Underground Station and in front of the Thames. The bazaar of politics, swirling with MPs, staff, visitors, journalists, gossip and intrigue.

Question Time: this is where the speechwriter's artistry comes into force, with pithy, caustic zingers, searching questions and clips for social media. Not just Prime Minister's Questions on a Wednesday, but also departmental questions to ministers each week.

Second Reading: when a bill's main principles and content are debated, with speeches from both front benches, party spokespeople, and backbench MPs.

Speaker: the person in charge.

Standing Orders: the rules of the game in a handy blue book.

Ten-Minute Rule Bill: this is a type of Private Members' Bill with a ten-minute speech by a backbencher, and another one opposing it.

Time Limits: when the Speaker imposes a time limit on a speech, meaning that speeches must have some elasticity to adapt.

Treasury bench: the front bench where government ministers sit (not just Treasury ministers).

Tricolon: things in threes. Don't ask why. They just work.

Urgent Questions: this is when a minister is hauled into Parliament by MPs on a topic in the news. The Speaker decides on the day whether to wreck the minister's schedule and throw speechwriters into a last-minute panic.

Usual Channels: the working relationship of the whips from the different parties and the leaderships of the government and opposition parties. A major part of the hidden parliamentary wiring.

Westminster Hall: is the medieval hall that has survived fire, flood and blitz, where the Queen lay in state, where Mandela addressed both Houses, and where Charles I was tried for treason. Up the stairs in the corner is the Grand Committee Room used since 1999 as a debating chamber. Here 'Westminster Hall debates' take place.

ABOUT THE AUTHOR

Paul Richards is a speechwriter, author, broadcaster and trainer. His first paid political job was in Parliament in 1991 as a policy adviser to a member of the shadow Cabinet, and he has worked in and around Parliament ever since. Paul was a special adviser to the previous Labour government, in three departments, under two Prime Ministers.

Paul has been a parliamentary candidate at the 1997, 2001 and 2024 general elections and candidate for Police and Crime Commissioner in Sussex in 2021 and 2024.

He serves on the executive of the Fabian Society and has written multiple Fabian pamphlets and articles. His books include a collection of Tony Blair's speeches and articles, entitled *Tony Blair in His Own Words*, and a guide to using the media, titled *How to Be a Spin Doctor*.

Paul Richards holds an MA in Victorian Studies (with distinction) from Birkbeck, University of London. He is a member of the UK Speechwriters' Guild, the National Union of Journalists (NUJ), the entertainment union Bectu, the Reform Club and Ronnie Scott's.

He lives in Eastbourne with his family, in Sussex by the sea.

FURTHER READING

This is just a small smorgasbord of books I recommend on the topics of Parliament, language and speechwriting. For the mechanics of speechwriting and speechmaking, there is none better than Max Atkinson's *Lend Me Your Ears*. He coached and wrote for many politicians over many years, including Paddy Ashdown. Max died in 2024, aged eighty. May he rest in peace.

Lend Me Your Ears by Max Atkinson
Parliament: The Biography, vols. I–II by Chris Bryant MP
When They Go Low, We Go High by Philip Collins
The Art of Speeches and Presentations by Philip Collins
She Speaks: The Power of Women's Voices by Yvette Cooper
Ghostwriting by Andrew Crofts
Bloomsbury Quotations for Speeches ed. John Daintith
How to be a Parliamentary Researcher by Robert Dale
The Lost Art of the Great Speech by Richard Dowis
The People Speak: Voices that Changed Britain by Colin Firth and Anthony Arnove

Punch & Judy Politics: An Insiders' Guide to Prime Minister's Questions by Ayesha Hazarika and Tom Hamilton

On Writing by Stephen King

Honourable Insults: a Century of Political Invective by Greg Knight

You Talkin' to Me? Rhetoric from Aristotle to Obama by Sam Leith

Write to the Point by Sam Leith

Speechmaking: The Essential Guide to Public Speaking by Susan Jones

The Penguin Book of Historic Speeches ed. Brian MacArthur

The Penguin Book of Modern Speeches ed. Brian MacArthur

Politics and the English Language by George Orwell

Speeches that Changed the World by Simon Sebag Montefiore

Eloquence: A Treasury of Speechwriting Advice ed. UK Speechwriters' Guild

ALSO BY PAUL RICHARDS

BOOKS

How to Be a Spin Doctor: Handling the Media in the Digital Age

How to Win an Election: The Art of Political Campaigning

Tony Blair: In His Own Words

Labour's Revival: The Modernisers' Manifesto

PAMPHLETS

Long to Reign Over Us?

Is the Party Over? New Labour and the Politics of Participation

The Case for Socialism: New Labour and the 'S-word'

INDEX